Journey
through Uncertainty
& other short stories

Edited by P. Comley

Ouen Press

Copyright © 2017 Ouen Press and contributors

All rights reserved. No part of this book may be reproduced in any form without permission from the publisher except for quotation of brief passages in reviews.

The moral right of the contributors has been asserted.

Published in Great Britain in 2017
by Ouen Press

Suite One, Ingles Manor, Castle Hill Avenue
Folkestone, Kent, UK
www.ouenpress.com

ISBN: 978-0-9956299-3-6

A CIP catalogue record of this book is available from the British Library.

Cover Design: Ouen Press, Main illustration: istock/cherezoff

With thanks to
everyone who helped
make this project happen.

CONTENTS

Foreword	i
Emma Smith – Journey through Uncertainty	1
John Frew – Danny on the Beach	19
Sophia Jackson-Gill – The Land of the Free	37
S.R. McGlynn – Journey to Everywhere	63
Valerie Horton – Into the Blue	89
Robbie Gilmore – Canoeing on the Hudson	107
Aviva Dale Martin – Manuela	141
Preview: Flights of Fancy by Michael Connor	169

FOREWORD

As has been said before, and we don't mind repeating here – we believe the short story offers a brief respite from the always-on culture of the multi-media environment. It allows a tiny escape, a small investment of focus, to be rewarded by a bountiful gift that salvages or invigorates the imagination.

The contributors to this compilation include the successful winner, runners-up and commended entries of the 2016 Ouen Press short story competition. This anthology is less about the detail of travel and more about embracing the possibilities to experience – physically, of course, but also emotionally, psychologically, or even spiritually, depending on your belief system. The theme of the competition invited contributors to consider and relate how they might have been changed by a 'journey' – an encounter that allows us the time to reflect on the world, on ourselves and to reinforce or challenge our viewpoints.

And so our writers have journeyed all day, but not moved very far – have taken circular routes, finishing where they started – but have broadened their view far more than they ever thought possible. Some have been challenged by seemingly insurmountable natural obstacles, only to find the wherewithal inside themselves – humour, courage, physical and emotional strength – to reach above and beyond their own expectations and those around them. In all, there have been realities contemplated and revealed, and life-lessons learned.

Congratulations and thanks go out to those whose work is contained herein, providing their testimony to an event, a place, a time, a sentiment. It is clear that telling the tales of the journey helps to convey meaning and assists understanding. Without such an account, some journeys may never be understood. We can be left bewildered, bereft of an explanation of its importance to the traveller and ignorant of its value to us. A perspective on a place or experience is an opportunity to live in the moment of another's anticipation, frustration, fear or elation – and take from it whatever information or knowledge we can or need at that time.

As a gift of time and thought, this collection holds the possibility for the reader to be inspired, enlightened or entertained – maybe all three!

THE PRIZE WINNERS

EMMA SMITH

Emma Smith lives in Wicklow, Ireland where she is surrounded by fields and mountains, heather and gorse. Emma loves heading outdoors with her crazy and excitable dog, and being in the midst of whatever nature and the Irish weather throw at her.

At home, two teenagers create enough havoc to keep her on her toes. She's counting down the days until they can drive, so she can shut down the 'Mammy taxi' for good. Emma has a lovely husband, Steve, who just wants her to be happy. He claims to get a bad rap in her writing.

Emma belongs to Dunlavin Writers' Group, which meets for long rambling discussions about life, and beyond. It's like therapy, but cheaper, with lots of coffee and great stories to be shared.

She has gathered two Master of Arts degrees, helped along by her ability to write and write. But after many years of business writing and online editing, she now writes her own stuff. She says it's the most challenging thing she's done. Keeping her sane – mostly.

WINNER
OUEN PRESS
SHORT STORY COMPETITION 2016

JOURNEY THROUGH UNCERTAINTY
by Emma Smith

My journey was but a short one. 1500 metres in length and just over thirty minutes to complete. It took place in the Upper Lake of Glendalough or Gleann Dá Loch, *which means valley of the two lakes. This is my story...*

I gasped loudly and repeatedly as a trickle of ice wound its way inside my wet suit. It spread across my body. Nipples jerked to attention. I dived and saw for the first time the dark brown nothingness below. My heart pounded noisily in my chest. I spluttered to the surface shaking myself like a wet dog flinging water from its body.

Head reeling from the impact of the cold, this was no gentle immersion in a heated swimming pool. This was an icy body of dark water and, except for six large buoys marking the course, there was no friendly line of floats to guide me. No well-lit tiled floor or coloured wall to turn at. The start of this swim was no dive into a clean chlorinated blue, but a chilling walk from the gritty shoreline, through the shallows, then a swim out to the start. The start line was indistinct – only roughly marked by the plethora of swimmers who bobbed in a straggling line out from a small green float.

I turned to face the lake proper and spotted the first marker, a big yellow buoy incongruous against the peaty darkness of the water and the heathered mountains beyond. I was still contemplating this, still coming to terms with being in this lake for this swim, when a loud horn reverberated around the valley walls and every swimmer in the water took their first stroke. We were off.

o0o

This steep sided valley with its long slick of

water drew me back time and time again. In the sixth century AD, a monastic settlement grew up around St Kevin who found his retreat from the world here. In the valley, schist-stone buildings still stand centuries later. In my own way I absorbed something of its atmosphere. I remember trailing my fingers along the lichen-covered walls as I craned my neck to find the top of the tall, round tower – a landmark still, in this ancient place. Or, peering through the metal grill into the dark interior of the ancient refectory.

Many times, I walked the Miner's Trail past the lake. I remember a heron standing one-legged in the wash where Poulanass River spews out into its waters. And the shaggy feral goats that ignored my panting efforts as I climbed higher. Then turning onto the mountain-top boardwalk, where antlered deer grazed the sparse bracken, and I could see the vertiginous drop to the valley floor where the upper lake lay. In the distance, the Irish Sea merged with the horizon.

I could understand why St Kevin built his hermitage on a cliff-face looking out over the lake. Embraced by tall mountains on three sides, the lake was both serene and mysterious. Sometimes a mountain breeze ruffled the waters into small lapping waves. Other times an eerie calm created a mirror-like reflection of tall firs and mountains.

Yet I always felt there were limits to what I could experience. For most of the year the lake is left untouched – no boating or swimming allowed.

o0o

It was a simple thing in March 2015 to click on a screen and book my place. The swim was equivalent to about sixty lengths of a twenty-five metre pool. I could do that. Of course, that's in nice warm water. But I had a few months to train and build stamina. It felt right. I signed up there and then.

But on the day as I stood silently to the side of the noisy crowd, I couldn't remember why I had signed up for this. I couldn't appreciate the history or the setting that always attracted me there. I wasn't laughing or cracking jokes. My stomach churned and grumbled – accompanying the panicky flutter inside. Did I have my wetsuit on properly? Would my goggles fill with water? Just how cold was the lake?

There were some serious looking dudes here. All kitted out in superfine triathlon suits, some with fleece-lined coats over them to keep warm. They were rangy, tall and fit-looking. I didn't see the others like me. They were probably there. Cowering quietly, as I did, feeling ill-prepared and unsure. And definitely not skinny and ready-for-anything looking. For that was not me.

Why had I signed up for this? Why was I trying to prove to myself, or anybody, that I could do it? And worse still, what if I couldn't?

My husband was with me, doing support. He was holding my drink and carrying my towels, and basically not knowing where to put the stuff or what to say. I should've been grateful. I was, I think. But he didn't understand. Didn't get this need in me. Wondering what had got into me, I suppose.

How can I explain what began like an irritating itch? A nagging discomfort that grew into feeling that I'd somehow forgotten myself. It was surely a contrary feeling. Shouldn't I be happy with all that I'd achieved? A home? A marriage and children? Good health? But this contrariness asked to be recognised and it didn't celebrate the life I'd made. It wanted something else. And it was very insistent.

oOo

A blur of yellow. I passed the first buoy. Over to the left, a flurry of swimmers swept by. It vividly reminded me of a flock of starlings startled by the garden-cat. Their energy was frenetic and fast. I could not hope to keep up. Maybe they had a plan that I was not part of. Perhaps the group created it's own momentum. Slipstreaming one behind the other. The lead swimmers cutting a path through the resistant water, easing the way for the followers.

My plan – if I had one – was to swim as straight as I could from buoy to buoy, and to try to finish. That was it. I had nobody to discuss strategy with. I wasn't thinking about times or personal bests. I had read up on open water swimming just to get some advice. So I knew that I had to try to keep heading for each marker and to try not to veer off course. This meant keeping an eye on the yellow buoys as I swam. It meant interrupting the natural rhythm of the swim, but a necessity if I wanted to avoid travelling further than needed.

So on one of my head turns to breathe, I popped up higher to sight the second buoy. It seemed far away as if it was a small cork bobbing in a giant bath. The buoys were much further apart than they looked from the shore. Now that I was at water level, I found it hard to believe I would manage to pass all six of these great hulking things – let alone get to the second. With a grunt I put my head back, rotating one arm after the other. My hands cut through the icy cold, pulling back hard and propelling me forward.

A black suited sleek-skinned body brushed up beside me as if sidling up to me in some sleazy nightclub. I half expected the whiff of drink. Yet just as it moved against me, it left me. Then I became aware of a foot fluttering periodically against my thigh. Disconcertingly, I could see no connecting body. Next a flash of pink announced another visitor. Her arm, when she belted out her moves, stroked me as intimately as a lover. Caressing me. Something else – an elbow or a knee - poked me in the ribs, rudely it felt.

These nameless bodies encroached on me. The faceless moving entities spreading apart and then coming together. Carried it seemed, on some incoming and outgoing tide, with its own horrible unknowable energy. I didn't want them. I felt my hackles rise, suddenly furious that I had to put up with it. With a deep breath, I pushed myself away. Dragging my arms through the water to emerge free from them. Alone again.

With breath after breath, and stroke after stroke, the next yellow buoy was no longer a small blip in the distance but sat tall on its long tether to the bottom of the lake. Bigger and bigger in my glimpses of it until it soared above me like a great nodding head as if to say: 'Yes! Yes! That's it. Keep going.' I passed it by. Two markers down and four to go.

The next buoy represented the apex of the swim. At that point I would turn and cross the lake and would finally begin my return. I found myself in a nice rhythm, one that I'd practiced in the pool. Three strokes breathing to the left, then a double stroke face down to switch sides, followed by three strokes to the right. My technique was working. And for a few minutes, I swam relaxed, looking up now and then to make sure the next buoy was ahead, then settling back into my swim.

The high imposing cliffs surrounding the lake rose sheer from the waters. Did they extend, I wondered, into the lake to plunge quickly and relentlessly down? I certainly could see no bottom and hadn't since I stepped off the green mat walkway leading into the water at the start of the race. Once that ended, it was like I had dropped off the edge and entered a large and silent space below. It felt deep.

But I shouldn't mind that. I'm a good swimmer. My hands, cutting through the silty brown, looked clean and bright and purposeful to me. I swam on.

Bubbles floated towards me from the chasm below. How were they made? What creature passed below, silent and hidden? I thought this lake was inhospitable to fish due to the old lead mines up by the Poulanass River. However I reminded myself that was a long time ago and probably there were fish aplenty now. At the same time, this lake may have things that exist here that are never seen. I suddenly felt small in this great expanse of water. As insignificant as a leggy pond-skater eking out a life, skitting hither and thither. At any moment to be taken for a meal by the lurking predator below. My heart gave a thump.

I forced myself to look instead to the views visible on each breath – the tall trees that lined one side of the valley, the rocky foreshore – and welcomed the third yellow buoy as I came up on it, suddenly converging with a group as they all rounded the marker together. From being on my own I was now surrounded by swimmers. I was level with one man for some time as we crossed the width of the lake, heading for buoy number four.

We eyed each other on each breath. I felt as if it was now me who invaded the man's space. Like a dead fish-eye, he stared at me blankly. It was cool, unwelcoming and very close. We swam in sync for a few moments and I couldn't do much about it but to keep on swimming. Finally, I turned away from my companion's glare and in the distance could just make out the big inflatable blue and yellow finish arch. I could see the beach and the small people on the shore waiting our return.

I wondered about my husband. Was he standing there scanning all the matching green swim-hats? Wondering which swimmer I was? Had he the towels and camera ready? What did he think about my mad adventure? Was this the man I'd married all those years ago? Was he wondering all this or was it just me?

He was no longer the young man I'd met and married that was for sure. He was less quick to have a laugh these days. There was a vagueness to him. As if he wasn't all there. Half the time he seemed quite exhausted by life. Whereas I felt like tearing it up, ripping it asunder and throwing all the pieces into the air. To see where they landed perhaps.

I reached the fourth buoy. It should have been welcome. It meant I turned for the finish. But other swimmers turned with me. They churned the water and seemed to move as one. A great big mass of arms and legs kicking and slapping. Passing the buoy provided no relief as the previous markers had done. The water tossed and turned with the maelstrom of swimmers making it impossible to get a clean breath. I gasped and swallowed water. My arms flailed uselessly, trying to find a calming rhythm but it evaded me.

I tried to see the next buoy. This would give me a goal to aim for. But all I could see was the splash and chaos of the group. My heart protested. Great big exploding beats of complaint. I tried again to find the marker. I was desperate now. Feeling lost if it wasn't in my sights. But failing to see it, all I could do was to follow the other swimmers.

They moved as one – a shoal of fish in their determination. This more than anything seemed to say they were right. I followed but that meant staying with the upset and confusion. I swallowed more water and choked.

This time I stopped dead. My arms dropped and I treaded water for a moment. The group moved off, leaving me behind. I watched them go. They knew what they were doing. Intent on where they were going. A focused assault on the lake that together they were taming. Conquering it, so it seemed. And safety in numbers, I imagined. They weren't bombarded by insecurity, by questioning, and by doubts.

I wanted to get out of the water now. I knew I simply had to raise my arm and one of the rescue kayakers would be with me in a moment to guide me out.

I took a deep breath. Closed, then opened, my eyes. I would try for a bit longer. Just a few strokes. I forced myself to swim. But after three or four strokes I halted again. I could just stop. It would matter to no-one but myself. Why did I need to go on?

But I had been working towards this for so long. This mad inexplicable thing, I, myself alone, decided to do. Something I'd trained for. To prove to myself that I could do this. To be alive to the possibilities of this life. If I gave up now...

For a few seconds I bobbed in the water. Outstretched arms making small circles as the cool silky water lapped my fingers. My body upright in the water with my feet kicking gently.

No revelation came. No beam of light. No words either. In fact there was no more thinking. And there was no more doubt. Just doing. A deep breath. A flick of my feet. I put my face down and this time I kept on going. Not dwelling on what was ahead but simply concentrating on each stroke, each breath, each swing of my arm and kick of my leg. My breathing came back to a rhythm I could maintain.

The lake opened up a space around me. It gave me room to breathe and stretch out. I closed my eyes and for a few moments felt the peace of the place – its great depths, its soaring heights – surround me. I felt it as part of me. I swam with a well-controlled rhythm. A beautiful coordination of body, limbs, breath and soul. It was elegant. With barely a ripple, I skimmed the water. I got to the fifth buoy.

Far out to the left a fellow swimmer swam alongside. Like swans in flight we swam in unison. An orange kayak glided along with us. It was silent and serene and the comfort I felt from their presence was almost profound. The sense that I was not alone but that there was help where it was needed.

Not that I needed it now. I knew I could do it. I reached the final buoy and turned to spot the finish. There, standing jubilant on the shore was the big finish arch and I headed towards it. My companion swimmer swam towards me and got ahead. The sun came out and was blinding. The last challenge of the day. But I didn't mind. I simply let the bubbles created by my companion's feet guide me to the end.

I hauled myself up and out of the deeper water, splashing through the shallows but feeling off balance as if the ground was no longer firm under foot. I swayed, and like a soda bottle shaken until it couldn't take the pressure, a great gurgle of emotion erupted from within. I whooped in delight, pulling my hat and goggles off and shaking my head, droplets flying from my short hair.

The swimmer in front of me turned and grinned. We embraced. Other swimmers were leaving the course behind us so we parted; my companion swimmer walked ahead and was lost in the crowd of supporters.

I walked out of the water through the giant arch, where there was cheering, hugging, laughter.

I had done it. I had really done it. But my

head now swam. Coming from the water after such an effort, I was disorientated. I felt alone in the noisy crowd. I looked around wildly. I didn't know where to go. I didn't know who to turn to.

Then a hand grasped me, steadying me. I looked up and there he was. He squeezed my arms tightly.

'You did it! You did it!' he repeated.

His eyes shone as he gazed at me. He could not stop grinning. Eyes creased, cheeks aglow, his hands holding on to me. Oh! But I loved him for that. Loved him brightly. And I clung to his shoulders, still gasping, still dizzy.

JOHN FREW

John Frew was born in 1986, and grew up in Cheshire, in the North West of England. He worked for the UK government for several years as an adviser on economics and trade, and completed a diplomatic posting at the British Embassy in Myanmar in 2013-14.

He left the Civil Service in 2016 and began a series of pilgrimages in different religious traditions in Europe and Asia. The events in his story 'Danny on the Beach' took place at the end of one of these pilgrimages, after walking 350 miles from Lisbon, Portugal to Santiago de Compostela, Spain on the Camino de Santiago or 'Way of St James'.

John is currently working on his first book, based on another walking pilgrimage in Myanmar, between the city of Mandalay and the Golden Rock pagoda.

When not travelling, he lives and works in south London.

RUNNER-UP
OUEN PRESS
SHORT STORY COMPETITION 2016

DANNY ON THE BEACH
by John Frew

I bumped into Robbie on the way to the station. His coffee had just arrived, and he asked if I would sit with him. I started to say no, I didn't have time – but something stopped me, and I sat down too.

He told me I seemed a little sad. I said, 'reflective'. It's funny how the two end up being more or less the same thing. Robbie seemed reflective too, but I didn't feel I needed to point it out.

I told him where I was going, and why. He nodded sagely. I didn't explain that it was all an accident – that I had arrived here at the end of my pilgrimage just the day before Alastair's thirtieth, all by chance. The coincidence seemed too absurd to mention.

The café was busy, and it was hard to get hold of a waiter to pay the bill. Robbie did the British thing, speaking loud and slow in English. The waiter struggled with the thick Glaswegian accent, and never came back. So I went in to pay. When I came back, Robbie took my hand in his two massive paws. He hoped I would make the most of my life. I said I hoped he got a little longer than he expected. He didn't respond, and I realised what a terrible thing I had said. I left for the station.

When I first met Robbie he was drunk, and drinking. A couple of hours later I got back to the pilgrims' hostel after dinner. He was on his way to bed. My friend Ellen sang something in the dormitory next door before we settled down to sleep. As she was finishing, Robbie appeared in the doorway and asked if she knew *Danny Boy*. It reminded him of his brother, he said.

Two hours later, Ellen had sung *Danny Boy* six or seven times. Ellen was a trained opera singer who taught music in Chicago, and she entertained us most evenings. She sang Joni Mitchell, and Jeff Buckley, and for Paolo she sang Fabrizio d'André. But that was the only night she sang *Danny Boy*.

It reminded Robbie of his brother, who had died alone on the streets of Southampton. Robbie had shifted everyone downstairs, and then gone out to buy more wine. He could only get it from a bar, and it cost more than he would have liked but, he said, 'you canna take it with you.' So he had me pour full glasses for everyone, and then he asked Ellen if she knew *Danny Boy*.

Robbie was very nearly just the hostel bore. Except that his brother had died alone on the streets of Southampton. He was very nearly just the hostel bore, except that he had been thrown from foster home to foster home throughout his childhood, and he cared about helping other kids avoid the same upbringing. He was nearly the hostel bore, except that he still had the scars from the police beatings he had incited on purpose to get the Scottish Socialist Party some publicity in the 70s. He was nearly the hostel bore, except that he had dedicated his life to helping people. He was nearly the hostel bore, except that at seventy-one he was making a pilgrimage of hundreds of miles to Santiago, for the thirteenth time in his life. He was nearly the hostel bore, except that he had lung cancer, and didn't expect to see Christmas.

We weren't going to bed until both bottles were finished, and nobody else was drinking. So I kept going, glass after glass. Ellen could barely keep her eyes open. She hunched, exhausted over her ukulele. But she sang *Danny Boy* every time he asked. It reminded him of his brother. He had died alone on the streets of Southampton, a penniless drunk.

o0o

At five the next morning, Robbie was gone. I hadn't seen him again on the way. But now here we were, in Santiago, three weeks after leaving Lisbon. My first time, his thirteenth.

I hoped he got a little longer than he expected. What a thing to say.

'I hope you don't die as soon as you think.'

He gave me a strange look, and I left for the station.

On the train to La Coruña, I wrote my letter to Alastair, and folded it into a little paper boat. I tried to say the right things this time. I had another piece of paper, one with a pilgrim's prayer printed on it that I had found in a chapel in the cathedral. I folded that into a boat as well.

The bus to Sada went all the way round the coast, up the peninsula and down again. At each fishing village I wondered if we were there yet. A grey-haired lady in the seat in front told me not to worry. She would point it out. Sada was very beautiful, she said.

It was gone two in the afternoon by the time we arrived. I wandered up and down briefly, and then went into a restaurant that stood alone on the promenade. It was built from timber and glass, a magnificent relic from some bygone age, with the paint peeling from the wood. Rows of tables marched like phalanxes of pawns down the chequerboard floor. The waitress was friendly but nervous. Nobody else was there.

I sat outside, against her advice, and then came in when it started raining. I tried to order a bottle of wine with my octopus, but she could only assume I hadn't understood where the half-bottles were on the menu. I gave up in shame, and had a half-bottle. The octopus was fresh and tender, served in fragrant olive oil and dusted with paprika. I was suddenly conscious of the way it had been hacked to pieces. The pieces lay there, half-animal, half-alien, and all dead. I ate every last scrap.

The marina was quiet: boats packed tightly along the jetties, but no people to be seen. I found the harbourmaster's office, a little cabin set slightly apart, but it had shut at three-thirty. I wandered aimlessly, looking for someone to ask. Eventually a young man in orange overalls returned from one of the jetties, and I told him what I was looking for. He said he wasn't sure, but he would try to help. He shrugged off my apologies for my bad Spanish, and led me to the offices of the Yacht Club. I had tried them once already and they looked deserted, but he shouted upstairs and a woman came down. She was kind and dignified; she didn't pry, but she asked gently for the information she needed, and made me repeat the name of the boat a couple of times.

'Golden Down?'

'No, *Golden Dawn.*'

'Down?'

'No, *Dawn*... como se dice? Aurora? Alba?'

'Ah! Amenecer? *Dawn*? Yes, yes. Oka-ay.'

She checked the records on her computer, but there was nothing there. It didn't seem to matter anyway. I had an image of some great heavy book, a harbourmaster's log with big, well-thumbed pages, alphabetical tags, off-white paper. Seeing the entry on a computer screen wouldn't have been the same.

There was another sailing club just along the way. She told me to try there, but wasn't sure their records would go back far enough. She was right. They took my phone number in case they found anything, which was impossible, but a kind gesture.

It seemed odd that there was no trace left. I thought information lasted forever now. I thought it was impossible to disappear, that everything was kept on file somewhere, by someone, for some purpose, or for none at all. Not here. It was as if the *Golden Dawn* had never been here at all.

o0o

In the Carrefour, I stood undecided for a while between the champagne, and the cheap cava at two euros fifteen. The cava seemed like the right thing. *It's what he would have wanted.* But it was his thirtieth, and I didn't want to feel like I was being cheap. I took the champagne from the shelf, and hid it in a freezer cabinet to cool down for a while, underneath a packet of churros. I didn't know you could get frozen churros.

I explored a little more while I was waiting

for it. In the same building there was some kind of working-men's club. Dozens of men sat with small glasses of beer at canteen tables, playing cards. The walls were all made of glass, but I was afraid to catch anybody's eye. I stood at the end of a jetty, taking deep breaths. The harbour smelt bright green – it smelt Atlantic. Eventually I went back to retrieve the champagne, and took it to the beach.

The beach was quiet. Two couples lay out on towels, fully-clothed under the overcast sky. A skinny young man in swimming shorts was marching up and down in the shallows. He never stopped or changed his pace. He must have marched the length of the beach twenty times while I was sitting there. There was a fat middle-aged lady, too. She stomped about aimlessly for a bit, and then lay down flat in the shallows. The skinny man kept on marching, full of purpose. The woman splashed half-heartedly, and then got out.

I had been there for about an hour when I became conscious of the wind on my face, and realised for the first time that it was blowing straight onto shore. I looked with dismay at the two little paper boats sitting on the sand in front of me. I was half-way through the bottle of champagne. I took it with me into the shallows, and tipped a little champagne into the sea. I didn't think about it too much. I had already pissed in the sea as well. I didn't think about it too much.

Remembering, it turns out, isn't really an activity. That's why we have ceremonies, poems, and special prayers to read. Otherwise, it's not very clear what you're meant to be doing. I thought about Alastair, and tried to imagine him here. I tried to imagine what he was thinking when he was here, but of course it was pointless. He didn't know what was about to happen. What was there to think about? Remembering, it turns out, is not a good way to fill an afternoon. I picked grains of sand from the raw surface of my walking blisters. I was glad I had brought my book.

A little before six, the wind changed, and the sky began to clear. I went down into the water again with the two paper boats, the letter and the prayer, and waded out until I was waist deep. I couldn't think of anything important or momentous to do, so I just put them in the water. They floated fine. I backed off quickly. If they tipped over, or got waterlogged and sank, I didn't want to be able to see it too closely.

Back on the sand, I watched them making

progress. They weren't going straight out to sea, but they weren't coming straight back onto the sand either. They bobbed away across the bay until they were two white specks. They probably wouldn't make it to Jamaica, but perhaps that was for the best. At least I wouldn't see them go under.

The sun was out now, and the warm evening seemed to bring the town to life. The promenade filled up with chatter, and whenever the wind turned to bring it to me, I knew that it was turning too to nudge the boats out into the bay.

Another woman was walking along the tide line, scanning the beach either side of her. She had hair the colour of rusting iron, and she was wearing a house-dress with green polka dots. I asked her what she was looking for, and she showed me a handful of cockle shells. She was going to cook them.

'They're hiding,' she told me. 'They all look empty, but some of them are full.'

At least, I think that's what she said.

Her cockle-picking gave me an idea, and before I left the beach I went looking for shells. Not cockles, but something else nice. I couldn't find a scallop shell, just a shard or two that hinted at one. There were some broken oyster shells too, but apart from that it was just mussels, clams and winkles. I collected a few clams, a couple of winkles and a bit of mother-of-pearl, and put them in my bag.

It wasn't dark, but already a few lights twinkled across the bay. I started humming something. *The pipes, the pipes are calling…*

A bus marked *La Coruña* pulled away when I was still fifty yards from the bus stop, but I waved, and the driver stopped for me further up the road. When I got on, he told me it wasn't the quickest route anyway, and pointed out the bus stop for a rival company that went direct.

I had a ticket for the nine o'clock train back to Santiago. When I had bought the return, I had said I would probably be coming back at six or so. But the man at the ticket desk had given me a ticket for the nine o'clock train anyway. He said if I came back sooner, I could always exchange it. It was just as well. The bus from Sada pulled up in La Coruña at eight forty.

I went into a small supermarket for a can of beer, and then I stopped to fill my water bottle at a drinking fountain. I fumbled, and dropped my things. One of the shells fell out of my bag, and skittered across the pavement. A little girl on rollerblades picked it up and handed it back to me. She had a very serious expression, a sort of benevolent admonition for my clumsiness.

When I got on the train, there was another little girl on the platform, about the same age. She was jumping around, waving, and blowing kisses to her mother, who sat just in front of me in the same carriage.

It was a relief to be back in Santiago. The ceremony was over. No more thinking about *what he would have wanted*. What would he have wanted? I could hear Claudia's voice in my head. 'Not to die, probably.' Probably.

I went for a steak, and had more wine with it. Again, the restaurant was empty. I had put aside the money for the bus to the airport the next morning, and I only just had enough money left to pay the bill. Alone on the streets of Santiago, a penniless drunk.

I used to have ideas about how, maybe, it was for the best. How, in a sense, it didn't matter whether he was dead or just disappeared: how this was his choice, and it wasn't our place to search for him. How maybe, he had met the romantic end he always secretly wanted. Finished it all, battling the elements on a raging sea, finally liberated from a world he never really got on with. Claudia didn't think so. She thought he would have gone down cursing his own foolishness, his own bad decisions, beating himself up just the way he always had done.

The investigators didn't think so either. Records said the weather was calm. He was crossing a busy shipping lane at night.

I wish I had been able to keep up the romantic illusion. But in the end it's probably always prosaic, dying alone. All the great adventurers, the explorers, faced down death any number of times. But they became great because they survived to tell the tale, so they got to tell it the way they wanted. They could tell it with embellishments and grand flourishes, or they could tell it with self-deprecation, understatement and British phlegm. Either way, it was their choice. Scott knew that, his frostbitten hands still scrawling with the last of his energy. You have to tell the story. Otherwise a firm of investigators will tell it for you.

It's probably always prosaic, dying alone. Ellen, I hate to ask you this – but do you know *Danny Boy*?

oOo

I woke up the next morning, gently

hungover. I had done my sums, and I had just enough money left for a coffee and the bus to the airport.

There was an indefinable feeling that stayed with me for days. It was a kind of dullness, as though I had never really sobered up. In the background, still, was the absurdity of my little rituals on the beach. Meanwhile, the family had their own celebration for him. I went along and sat, awkwardly, trying not to speak. I set myself up for a while behind the barbecue, my little fortress. When I did have to speak with people, nobody talked about Alastair. I thought information lasted forever. I thought it was impossible to disappear, that everything was kept on file. Not here.

I had the sense that I was failing at the game of remembering. It was exactly the sort of game, I realised, that would have enraged Alastair. He would have had the sense that he ought to be doing something, but he wouldn't know what the rules were, and he would be at a loss to find ways to express himself. He always was.

About a week later, I finally got round to unpacking my rucksack. I found the Carrefour bag from the beach, and the collection of shells in their bed of sand at the bottom of it. I shook them out onto the chest in my room. They lay there, small, matt and out of place. I tried to remember what I had thought I might do with them. I had some idea about handing them out to his family and friends – *collected from Sada, Alastair's last known landfall, on his thirtieth birthday, 4th August 2016.*

I took the biggest one in my hand, felt the surface of it with my thumb, not rough, but still textured. I put it back on the chest, a little further along. I swept the rest of them into my palm, and put them in the bin.

SOPHIA JACKSON-GILL

Sophia Jackson-Gill is an actor, writer and adventurer who, since graduating from The Birmingham School of Acting, has loved exploring the different platforms through which storytelling can be delivered.

She has co-written and made several short films and plays, one of which – *Untold* – was shortlisted for the Unchosen Film Awards 2013, and then used by the Greater London Assembly.

Her first attempt at creative writing was for the 2015 Brighton Fringe 500-word short story competition for the under-thirties, which was judged by Ali Smith. Sophia was one of the winners of this, and so her interest in creative writing began. Sophia is currently exploring the genre of television writing, continues to write short stories and, most importantly, is saving the pennies for her next inspiring adventure.

RUNNER-UP
OUEN PRESS
SHORT STORY COMPETITION 2016

THE LAND OF THE FREE
by Sophia Jackson-Gill

The sky stretches endlessly like a Dulux spillage in 'advert blue'. We drive – for hours, but it feels like minutes. Our wheels have taken off and we soar down the highway leaving Chicago's bite behind us. There is so much to see. Fall is as exquisite as the writers paint it. Trees dripping in yellow and dragon red, turning pixie green as we try to touch the sun. Three, four, five hours with no stops. No clunking jams threatening to sever our wings. We fly.

'Hell is real' – 'Jesus lives' – 'Guns save lives' – chain us to a reality that is theirs but not ours.

Yet another reminder, though we share a common tongue, we are not the same.

The golden arches on a school sign – adolescent obesity is owned by the corporates. Fast-food joints that glut the land in quantities that astound and make you question how, even in a country as vast as this one, there can be stomachs enough to warrant their existence? Food that will rot you from the inside out but barely alter the tune that plays out of your pocket change.

The road pushes on, arrogant in its refusal to deviate from its perfect path. We could go on forever, no turn-offs for us.

Nature's symmetry is mirrored on either side. There are no houses, trucks or animals, but giant signs proposing health-checks and better insurance are endless. Occasionally, a low-level building can be glimpsed between trees and almost always it is iced with a blue, red and white symbol of pride. Perilous and passionate in a triumphant wind. *'This country is great,'* it proclaims. I can hear it through the now greening leaves.

Over and over again we are tricked by signs that direct us to places that cannot possibly be sign-posted from here. Can the leaders of this *'free new world'* lack imagination so much that they name place after place, after place? The same recycled names from cultures and civilisations unacknowledged and replaced. Or is it simply that in a land this vast there comes a point where you cannot avoid re-treading old ground?

The real Indianapolis is a far cry from the canvas in my mind. We drive in circles searching for a brimming centre and are finally directed to a place that feels as though it has been comatose since 1952. It is reminiscent of a suburban *Mad Men* set with an eerie *Stepford* twist for good measure. Has our circling ripped open a gate to another dimension causing us to unwillingly slip in?

Across from our car is what seems to be a bowling alley. It's rife with an unfamiliar odour – sweet but with the hint of decay. A cage-lift beckons us, tiny and thick with dust. The concertina shutters slide and the lift wheezes into action, transporting us deeper into 1950s Indiana and it's duckpin bowling alley.

Lacquered floors and leather seats, hand painted *Cola* bins and pins that hang from their necks by strings. Worn but untouched. In east London this would be the epitome of cool, but here I am filled with unease. There is something stubborn and threatening in its refusal to evolve. Back at our *Super 8*, I shift towards you, until I am lying across your stomach. *Psycho* plays out in my mind.

The next morning we leave at daybreak. Flat plains give way to swooping land, enveloped in army-green firs that stand like ancient soldiers remembering a time when roads were unable to penetrate their loins. When we wind down the window to let in fresh air, it no longer claws and twists its way into the cracks of our skin but soothes and passes, not yet warming but letting us alone. We are on our way, like a twenty-first century Jack Kerouac but without the drama. Again the grating neon *'m'* flashes and flirts with us in an otherwise barren landscape. Maybe now it's as natural for this country as the rivers and lakes?

Nashville. Its heart beats to a country rhythm and reminds us that we are in the midst of musical genius here. B.B. is still King, Ike a God, and Dylan and Baez – living legends. Their songs were my lullabies, but I am far from home. I think of their words. How much has really changed in these sleepy towns?

Everywhere we step is an invisible line. No palette mixing here. I think of *'The Little Rock Nine'* and Rosa Parks. It wasn't so long ago. I thought more would have changed. It hasn't. Two Kings went to sleep in Memphis and people make pilgrimages to both, but when we visit only one is booming with people, overflowing out of his house like an over-fed child. The other, still waiting to be discovered, remains patient for acknowledgment.

We stop in a Wal-Mart and it is as excessive as I had imagined. I love it. Basking in the opulence of marshmallows the size of my fist and concoctions I spent my childhood hearing about in *Sweet Valley High*. There is something seductive about it until you check yourself and acknowledge the vacuity of it all. I go to the till. I watch the woman in front of me as she swipes my carefully chosen produce. She is one of those people who smiles from the inside out; her face is like the centre of a tree trunk, it tells no lies. Life runs through the purposeful creases that travel across it, proof that she has lived where others have not, each line is a moment she has survived.

She sucks me in with a throaty chortle, the type that my granny had. It makes me feel loved. We begin to talk about Memphis. She has always lived in this town, has never left. I think of all the places I have been to, countries I have explored. Then she begins to talk and I realise that I could travel for a hundred years and never know all that she does. My mind is opened.

She wishes to give me a message.

'God created a Rainbow, a people rainbow.'

She tells me this as if I am small, but I am bigger than her. I think I read a book about this at school, or maybe it was a film. I listen. She tells me that long ago, before her spine began to curl and her trunk grew thick, she had marched beside the King. I don't believe in God but if I did, my only certainty would be that Martin Luther King would sit out his days by the side of the Almighty One himself. Here I am in Wal-Mart having a piece of history thrust upon me by someone who lived it. This would never happen in Tesco.

It was a Thursday and her mamma had sent her to the shop around the corner on an errand. She should have been home by now but the kaleidoscope of candy had seduced her. She loved the way it looked, lined up in the glass jars, all neat and ordered and so full of promise. She had some change in her pocket and the possibilities were endless.

She had jumped when she heard the shot, like you do when something shatters your peace, not on the outside but in your marrow.

They had known immediately; it had been imminent. They say he told his wife when J. F. Kennedy was assassinated that he would be next. When my Wal-Mart cashier had heard the shot, she had tried to run to it. The shop owner had held her back, locked the doors and closed the blinds. She was going nowhere. They sat in silence for a long while listening only to the thud of their blood as it pumped around their bodies.

Finally the telephone rang. Martin Luther King was dead.

I feel the tears welling up in my eyes, which although not unusual for me, feels strange because I am in Wal-Mart and because I do not know this woman or her story. This man changed the world but not, I am just beginning to realise, by enough. Equality is illusory – equality is fragile and barely there. Festering under the cracking concrete is a reality that even the most liberal of us often choose unwittingly to ignore.

She laughs again in her thick, throaty way.

'When people learn to love each other and see beneath the rainbow, then we can all be equal but now, no one sees the rainbow.'

We leave with our giant marshmallows and a sense of unrest and head towards Arkansas –

the Natural State.

Drops splatter across our bonnet, turning into a frantic and relentless attack. Stopping for gas is like wake-boarding down the Mississippi. By the end we are sodden and laughing. The rain is cathartic, it cleanses us of our responsibilities and turns us to ten – no rules to obey! Still the air is thick and tight.

We have driven forward but it feels like we have gone back to a time where the speed and reality of the life back home does not exist. We hire a cabin by a lake, which has the unease of an early Polanski – all wood and creaks, with crochet dolls pinned by their necks watching from the walls. The oven needs to be lit and wooden boards dance beneath my trainers – but I daren't take them off because I may need to run . . .

Here we will see the natural beauty they boast of. We will bathe in hot springs and listen as the leaves whisper and fall.

We climb until we can't breathe; in this moment we know we are alive. The fragility of life without complication. Clouds swallow our heads. They are not the soft ripples of tangible fluff I have dreamed of but instead are vapid swirls of vapour that leave us breathless yet free.

It is not hot so we have no urge to unpeel our conservative layers and leap, defenceless, into the lake. Besides, there may be footless reptiles slithering beneath that mossy membrane. I watch the pier until darkness has swallowed the sky and spat out a million stars I have never seen before. I hear the hop, skip and splash of yesteryear's contented visitors. My mind is alive here with the memories of things I have not seen. Not haunted, but lived in.

We leave having never seen another soul. Our cash left on the table, as instructed. They trust you here. We obey, because this is how their life works, and depart beneath a tantruming sky.

We skid along the waterlogged roads, wrestling to steer straight. They never end but turn into new roads in new places. Houses become caravans, become shacks and then huts. People live here. Arkansas, Louisiana, Mississippi. They are not as I have imagined. We are in another world from the one that HBO and Netflix have sold us. Where is the greedy, capitalist monster that brings countries to their knees?

The Cross remains. It penetrates homes, taking new and old forms. It has been constant since the start of our journey, but now it is obdurate. Churches stand side by side or have only a few buildings separating them. Their presence is an absolute certainty that holds such a twisted irony I find myself laughing. This place does what it wants and answers to no-one. It never has . . .

Soon the road is dry and our open windows invite a blast of breezy air. We need it now. We head to Jackson because of the song, because of our name, because it's a place we will never go to again. We stay one night and drink until we are drunk. It is a concrete city with out-of-town malls. We never did find its heartbeat but perhaps it is sacred and penetrable only for those who love it.

On to a place where life pulsates and rages through every crevice. A city, whose foundations are built with the bones and sweat of mad convicts and even madder enforcers. New Orleans, which sits upon a septic, stolen, swamp. This, for us, was love. It is a zesty bubble of life, detached from the states that surround and hold it by its relentless spirit, and a bridge on stilts that sits above a defeated swampland. It hydrates you with hot jazz and Cuban riffs that steal you into a euphoric haze. It is hedonism. With invitations to gorge on dripping Po' Boys and decadent Creole cuisine, nothing about this place is conventional or American. It is startlingly unique, and while we could spend our days stumbling, incoherent but content through the French quarter with an icy daiquiri in hand, there is more to know here.

We stay in the Garden District and while away our first day exploring the neighbourhood. Picture-book homes in rainbow colours, Halloween dripping from every one. Makeshift graveyards and haunted homes. We walk along, stopping for cocktails and local fried cuisine.

It seems compulsory here to sport a sleeve of ink; we wander into one of hundreds of tattoo parlours and become seduced by the possibility of having a permanent memory etched into our skin. Why not? We are in the land of the free and anything is possible. Even the corruption of a creamy-skinned girl from south London, who never even smoked a cigarette. The needle drags through skin. My forever. There is something about this place that makes you want to drown in it. I could stay here.

We join a swamp tour and, although it is hibernation time, we track alligators.

The Land of the Free by Sophia Jackson-Gill

Disrespectful of nature's rules, the guide spots a half-submerged creature and begins to pelt it with marshmallows. The 'gator remains pensive and tolerant as sugary missiles hit it over and over. How would I feel if I was subjected to this three times a day? The woman in front of me has sturdy little legs – I consider how satisfactory a meal she would be.

At a Cajun cooking demonstration, the chef makes and we eat. By the end I am positive that I can say New Orleans like a local but I am not sure that I can recreate her praline, which dissolves on the tongue like melted gold. Next to us are the types you pray won't sit next to you, though at the same time you want to unravel. She is a bottle-red, the kind that screams at you from every strand and lets you know who is boss. He has drink wrinkles like the man who sits in the corner of your local Wetherspoons. Their heads wobble from side to side suggesting they are either sick or have had a few jugs before this.

I know what is going to happen, I have been warned again and again not to engage in this conversation, and so I allow them to take you captive instead. Meanwhile, I engage the placid woman on my left in a chat that turns into miscarriage, IVF and divorce. She leaves herself bare to me in a way that not even my best friend has done. It is raw and brave and I don't know how we have got into this conversation. Again, I am reminded that appearance is vastly deceptive. I should know this by now. Every so often I am jolted from our intimate exchange by another of the flame-haired woman's ludicrous statements.

'Ya'll got Muslims with guns in parts of London that won't let ya'll in if ya'll not wearing a scarf.'

I have lived in London my whole life and have never been stopped, either physically or through fear, from entering a single part of it. London is everyone's – that is its beauty.

I should help you but I am not as capable of separating my emotions, as you are my husband – a master of diplomacy who has the ability to communicate even with those who live in another world from the one the pair of us frequent. I have visions of launching myself across the circular table and squeezing her pasty neck between my fingers until all her viperous beliefs have left. But this would not help. Her response is that our media needs to, 'sort it out'. They miss the point that it is their media feeding them these particular lies.

You deliver impressive statistics about the

number of deaths through gun crime in their country to illustrate the point, but she retaliates.

'Ya'll should all be able to defend yourselves on ya'll own homes. If I had a gun I'd go out and sure as hell shoot down all them dam Muslims.'

This is the South. It answers to no-one.

Katrina has barely permeated the centre of the city – the places that tourists visit have been patched and healed until it is difficult to believe she was ever here. It is not all like this though. Homes have still not been rebuilt; there are corners the relief fund never reached. The recovery seems – in our ignorant foreign eyes at least – to have been rebuilt in a discombobulated fashion where the white and rich have their homes back, but the black and poor do not. The feeling that was born in Memphis is growing again.

It is time to move. We head to Galveston, to hear her sea-waves crashing.

We pass a sign for Lake Charles and blast *The Band* from the speakers. The plum-black sky darkens and so does the driving. Texas – they sure as hell know how to put their foot down. Water saturates the land and reminds us that we are only temporary visitors on this earth. The rain will always come.

We drive along a coastal road where the homes are in the sky. They sit on poles and challenge the sea beneath them. I cannot comprehend how you could bear to live with such a constant threat of floods – that you make your home a nest. Humans are bound to the earth. I am a city girl, through and through.

We cross to Galveston on a boat, hauled through the water by rope. The island is not what I pictured, but coming in the aftermath of hurricane season may not be the best time to visit. Light is scarce and the trees slap their branches on the road. A foreboding wind screeches all around us.

We follow our disinterested Airbnb host to a desolate marina, remove our shoes and wade through water that skims our knees, suitcases above our heads. The pier that leads to the boat we have hired has drowned and only the tip of our toes finds it. What skulks in the blackened water beneath us? Our host switches on some fairy lights as we clamber on deck. Does she imagine these flickering twinkles can transform the perilous boat into an object of desire? She leaves and I swallow. This is not how I have envisaged our honeymoon. I secretly wonder if this is how we will die.

We lie down on the red silk sheet that half covers the triangular... bed. It's like *Nosferatu*. My heart is pounding, but more alarming, so is yours. We decide to go out, we need some perspective.

We drive along the car-less streets searching for signs of life. Despite being a Friday night, it's desolate. Finally, we find a place. The three other people inside induce in me an inappropriate level of elation. We ask them about Halloween.

'Halloween's not so big here.'

An American city that doesn't do Halloween is like an England that never rains – impossible. We mask our disappointment and try not to think about how we have headed here because we thought it sounded haunted. A prime place to experience Halloween American style – we thought.

Even on an adventure as vast as ours, mundane tasks such as brushing our teeth in the marina washrooms must be adhered too. I slap at my face, feeling the sting of yet another thirsty creature. It has been a long day. The ocean has risen again. Against our better judgment we wade through the water, which now grazes our groins, and clamber into our floating prison. A storm has begun. Lightning illuminates the room, turning our sheets blood red. The boat convulses beneath us – the thunder here is like a rampant beast jolting us from calm each time it rages. I wonder whether we will see the night melt into day? My back is clammy and my eye is throbbing. It must be nerves. From hour to hour the storm grows. We could leave, but how would we get ourselves and our luggage on to dry land?

Finally, the moon and sun trade places. We have survived. I am not sure if either of us slept, but we are certain that we will not stop here another night. My eye feels disconnected so I find a stained mirror. It is enormous. It wasn't nerves, but a ravenous creature from the washroom. The monstrosity on my eye could not have come on a better day. It is after all, Halloween!

Houston is next, but we visit NASA on route. Science is exhilarating; I think back to those unyielding school hours spent copying out irrelevant facts. If only this had been my classroom. My eye is now bulbous, indicative of an incubator ready for its contents to hatch. People are staring. Nobody asks, but it is clear what they think. Still they walk away.

We upgrade and down a bottle of wine. We

deserve it. After all, we have escaped a ship burial. I paint our faces – mine needs minimal work – and crawl up the main street, drinking a nitrogen slush puppy. I am half-way through my glass before I realise my mistake, but by now the alcohol has flooded through my veins and is disconnecting the signals from my brain. Before long, we are talking at people who do not wish to be spoken to about things that they feel are not our business. Memphis rattled us and an agitation has begun to swell. Surely this is not the same country that calls itself the land of the free?

We continue. Watching the NFL is a minefield, not the game but because of what adorns it. *'Build a burger'* competitions where children relay-race dressed as giant buns and half-pounders, cheerleaders that look as plastic as the food stuffed into every orifice of the venue, and that national anthem, sung over and over and over.

There is suspicion in people here. A stark difference to the trust we found in the Natural State. Our accents are suspicious. By the end of the game they are sufficiently intoxicated to befriend us anyhow, and although at first they believe us to be from a little known American state, soon they are requesting photos with the

Europeans. They have not heard of England and find the language barrier troublesome, but they load us with barbecued meat anyway.

Finally we are travelling in style, a hair-whipping, open-top Chevrolet in lipstick-red. We enter the state capital, Austin. A misplaced, musical Shangri-La caught in the midst of redneck country. A democratic stronghold walled in by a Republican suburbia. The live music capital of the world absorbs us and soon we are fluent in its infectious pulse. It is easy and missing some of the intricate layers that other places we have visited have. We enjoy its weightless simplicity. It's fun. *'Keep Austin weird'* is its adopted slogan. I don't particularly find it weird, but I like it. It has the vibe of east London or Venice Beach but without the burden of expense and pretence.

We hike to the top of an enormous hill and see the river below meander off into the Texan land. Along the shore are homes that make my eyes pop. This place has money. We watch two girls do yoga on top of a rock, the rays of sunlight engulf their bronzed bodies and I think back to the room I practise yoga in. Flanked by other sweaty bodies in an often-grubby studio, just off the Mile End Road.

We go to a gun range and after flashing our

ID they toss us weapons that can end a life in a single moment. I wonder if they have mistaken us for regulars? We stand shoulder to shoulder inside the range; the earphones barely dull the sound and my heart jolts with every shot. We choose a circle target; the others fire at headless bodies. My stomach churns. I hold the gun with both hands. It is cold to touch and heavier than I expected. This is alien to me and all kinds of wrong. I lift it and feel my pulse quicken before pulling the trigger. It kicks back hard – I didn't expect this. Rubbing the ache between my thumb and finger leaves a dusty sediment on my hands. I shoot again, and again, but a strangling anxiety consumes me. I can't stay here, everything feels wrong. Sweat is dripping between my breasts and my throat scratches. I can't find my breath and the room is pushing me under. I leave.

Outside in the car I am calm again but I can't shake the dread, which lays within me – guilty, dirty, heavy. I won't shoot a gun again I'm more powerful without it.

The end is nigh, so we surrender ourselves to Lonely Planet clichés. We eat Tacos for breakfast and plunge ourselves into a soundtrack of Austin's finest. Meat here is prepared with the precision of fine art. I am told that it drips from the bone in a smoky haze. Silence tells me it is worth the wait. We visit the Dance Hall and try to two-step. We are incognito and when the teacher – thinking the group is free of Brits and our closest neighbours across the channel – starts to talk of the 'charmless' French and 'plain rude' English, we laugh. So the overt niceties *are* just for tips!

Our adventure has awoken us, fuelled us and transported us. Thank God we didn't ask for pots and pans as wedding gifts. The people we love most have ignited us and removed the fragile veneer of our western equilibrium. We have shifted from the familiar to a place of fascination and discomfort. We all need this – it is good for our souls. The bubble we often joke about inhabiting is more real than even India had shown me. Nowhere is perfect, and although I am convinced that there is beauty in imperfection I am certain that just beneath the intoxifying matrix of the US, an eruption is imminent.

COMMENDED

S. R. McGLYNN

S. R. McGlynn (Rosie) was published in the 2013 Momaya Press competition with her story, *Song of Despair*. She self published her first novel, *Spellbound: The Politics of Doom* the same year, and is currently preparing her second novel for publication, which she was inspired to write following the Brexit vote.

As a mature student she studied for a degree in Russian at the University of Leeds, incorporating an extra year into her studies by accepting a teaching post in Russia. She has made several road trips across Eastern Europe, and even organised a convoy of humanitarian aid helping the children of Chernobyl and a

Polish orphanage.

Living in Russia, she seized many opportunities to explore life off the beaten track, which she described in her letters home. Some experiences were amusing, others heart-breaking, many inspiring – with risks lurking at every turn. Drinking champagne on ice takes on new meaning after you've stood ***on*** the River Volga in December sharing a bottle with friends.

'Russia is a fascinating country,' says Rosie, 'and although I once had to bribe my way out at the airport for lack of *boomahgy* (papers), if it's experience you're seeking, Russia certainly has more than her fair share to offer, passing in a moment but often lasting a lifetime.'

Following self-employment in the UK as a hypnotherapist, Rosie now cares for an elderly relative, using the time this affords her to write fiction, poetry, and enter writing competitions.

COMMENDED
OUEN PRESS
SHORT STORY COMPETITION 2016

JOURNEY TO EVERYWHERE:
SEVENTY SOVIET YEARS IN A DAY
by S. R. McGlynn

Boarding a train in Moscow, destination *'Everywhere'*, marks a single day that encompasses a lifetime. It's many years since that day and yet I'm still riding that railroad. We all are.

Like many travellers, I've known countless branch-lines and dead-ends. But ultimately these matter little. So long as you enjoy the view, the company, the hope, then the destination pales into insignificance. Even losing your way is only part of life's journey. The view changes constantly, and where you thought you were heading becomes less important the further you travel.

Unlike many youngsters these days, I'd never even left the UK for a holiday until the grand old age of twenty-six. And unlike the usual sun-scorched beach destinations, my first flight carried me to Moscow in December, where I experienced champagne on ice for the first time too. Okay, so the ice was three feet thick, beneath which flowed the river Volga – but conformity was never my thing.

While studying in England for a university degree in Russian, I spent a total of eighteen months in Russia. Employment beckoned and I found myself teaching English as a foreign language in return for lodgings and lessons in Russian. However, the best lessons were not to be had in the classroom – the Russian word *koshmar* means nightmare, but most of these experiences were to be had while fully awake.

On a scorching August day in 1998, leaving my fifteenth floor roost in a Moscow suburb, I thought of friends I would visit in Tver. This city is about one hundred miles north of Moscow, where I'd previously taught English – so I'd made this journey many times. Having negotiated my way across Moscow by bus and the Metro, I arrived at Lenningradski Vauxhal, the mainline railway station for services north to Kalinin – that is Tver to everyone except railways staff – Novgorod, and Lenningrad – or, St Petersburg to the rest of us. A degree of awareness, if not an actual degree in Soviet and Russian history, was essential when navigating Russia's railroads back then.

The coach service departed from outside the railway station. By road, the trip took about three hours; by rail it was anyone's guess. At nine o'clock I discovered I'd just missed a coach so, feeling adventurous, I opted to take the local *Electreechka* train. My hasty calculations told me that the next coach to depart from Moscow would arrive in Tver at practically the same time as the next train. Maybe this was a foolhardy assumption.

Buying a ticket was straightforward enough thanks to my university studies and previous employment in Russia. With time to spare, I wandered around the many kiosks buying food and drink for the trip. At the same time, I decided to replenish my diminishing stock of batteries for my aged Walkman, a move that I would later regret.

Standing at the end of the concourse, watching the trains come and go, I closely observed the platform sign indicated by my ticket. When trains approach, these electronic signs display the destination of that service. Otherwise they bear the standard word '*Vezdyeh*', which means 'Everywhere'. As a train approached my platform I waited for the sign to change, probably indicating Kalinin – today's Tver – but it didn't change at all. Needless to say this didn't stop hundreds of Russians from frantically boarding it, seeking the best seats and arranging their voluminous amounts of luggage. I managed to gain the attention of one old babushka to check if this was indeed the Tver train.

'*Ne znaiyu,*' she mumbled – 'I don't know'– before shuffling off and climbing aboard.

From this I surmised that that she was a reckless old dear who liked to board trains, the destinations of which she didn't know. Being somewhat more cautious, I decided to ask someone else and approached a man standing on the platform who was chatting to passengers through an open window. As he turned towards me I noticed the open bottle of beer in his hand. Too late. This young, unaccompanied woman, speaking excellent Russian, albeit with a foreign accent, already had his undivided attention. His friends in the carriage were quickly forsaken.

Aleksandr, or Sasha as he insisted I call him, was as difficult to shake off as dog hair. Once he'd established that English was my native tongue, he proceeded to tell me about a delightful English girl he'd met recently at Lenningradski Vauxhal. Did I, perhaps, know her? I laughed, such were my doubts. The UK population was fast approaching sixty million, and he wondered if I might know one person in particular. Then he told me her name. It was only the very same Cambridge student who had emailed me for advice on language courses in Russia. My expression opened a door, and Sasha let himself in. After all, he practically knew me, didn't he? We already had a mutual contact.

Under his advice I boarded the train, whereupon he sat opposite me, perhaps unable to keep his eyes off the rather low neckline of my dress. Sasha had already fulfilled his function but seemed incapable of understanding that I had no further need, let alone desire, of his company. I began listening to some Russian pop music on my Walkman and, in case this wasn't sending out a strong enough signal, I also extracted a novel from my rucksack. But Sasha wasn't going to fade into the worn upholstery. Several times he tried initiating conversation, but I remained resolute. Finally he took the hint, arose from his seat and shook my hand as he bid me goodbye.

A scholarly gentleman was sat beside me, also reading – the Russian traveller's favourite past-time. As I muttered *'Preedurak'* – 'Prat' – upon Sasha's departure, he expressed agreement and sympathy in broken English, before returning to his book and I to mine. Any misgivings about taking the train had departed along with my unwanted suitor, and I began to relax and enjoy the journey.

We had been travelling for less than an hour when the train rolled to a halt beside a bare and dusty platform: nameless, unserviced, and baking in over thirty degrees of humid summer heat. Having taken in the view beyond the window, my attention then focused on the scene within the train. The passengers were gathering their belongings and alighting – ALL of them – except yours truly who had clearly missed any announcement thanks to the lyrics of *Andrei Gubin, Ivanushki International* and *Blestyashchiye*, Russia's then equivalent of the *Spice Girls*. This was long before *Pussy Riot* arrived on the scene.

Like a cat trying to regain its composure

after missing its footing, I cautiously pursued the natives only to discover that my worst fears were coming true. In response to my query came the definitive answer.

'Etot poyezd dalsheh ne poidyot.' – 'This train is going no further.'

So there we were, three to four hundred passengers marooned on a concrete platform. The station and, more importantly, any facilities, were situated across eight railway lines with no bridge or subway to connect us. The natives were totally unperturbed and sat on their luggage drinking beer and eating snacks, awaiting rescue. At times like these you can do no more, so I joined them in their mid-morning respite, applying a little more sunscreen and taking comfort from the fact that this was August, not January. Minus thirty degrees Celsius when you're minus control of your situation would have been a far greater inconvenience.

After about half an hour a replacement train drew alongside our glaring strip of concrete and I followed the natives' lead, climbing aboard promptly to find myself a seat. It never occurred to me to check that the destination of this train was the same as the one we had been obliged to abandon. I was too preoccupied revelling in the delight of securing a soft seat; many *Electreechki* only had uncomfortable wooden slats for seats.

Beside me sat a typical matriarch, of which Russia has a generous supply. All around us her bags and packages were neatly arranged, and I figured she was returning from the family's country retreat, the *dacha*. Those bags would be full of berries and mushrooms, tomatoes, milk, eggs, smoked fish – all home produced or gathered from the endless Russian forests. A young man sat opposite us, staring out of the window. I heaved a contented sigh when finally we crept away from the nameless platform, satisfied that the occupants of this carriage posed no obvious threat to my personal safety. Russia, however, still had several trump cards to play.

Less than five minutes later we drew into a green and shady siding and stopped again. For half an hour we remained there, listening to the birch trees rustling outside with the onset of a summer storm. I no longer dared listen to my Walkman for fear of missing another vital announcement, not that I could usually make out a single word of these broadcasts at the best of times. To my knowledge, neither could most Russians, which is why they often seek clarification of these messages. They were sometimes so desperate they'd even ask me.

This latest halt lasted until an express whistled past, bound for Moscow. And finally, we got on our way. I was already counting the cost of failing to take the bus, which by then would have already arrived in Tver. Meanwhile I was still at the mercy of Russia's whimsical railway employees. My discomfort grew when I learned we had no facilities whatsoever on board this train and could only pray for a rapid arrival in Tver.

By now the glorious sunny day had given way to a summer storm of mammoth proportions. Thunder roared above the noisy clatter of the train and lightning tore through the gloomy carriage every few seconds, providing a momentary source of light for a few stalwarts still trying to read. Passengers began closing the windows as the rain lashed against the train and swept through the carriage, but I noticed how these windows were hinged at the base and opened a full 180 degrees. In order to fasten them shut, one would expect there to be a catch or bolt at the top, but had there ever been so, in Russia such precious bits of metal would have long-since been misappropriated. Consequently, as the train gathered speed for the first time and hurtled forward, many of these windows fell open with disastrous results. The young man sat on the opposite seat took such a blow to the head that it necessitated the matriarch's kind offer of a handkerchief to stem the flow of blood.

Gradually, as more and more injuries resulted, the windows were left open and the rain, together with the blood from a dozen wounds, gushed through the carriage like a torrent. One woman donned a plastic mackintosh, while I seriously considered putting up my umbrella. What would the Russians have made of that? Their superstitious nation may have castigated me for not sparing a moment to sit down and gather my thoughts before I embarked on this journey – an essential ritual for any self-respecting Russian – but would I be rebuked for simply trying to keep dry?

Fortunately the torrential shower soon gave way to sunshine once more. It was two o'clock by this time and still there was no sign of Tver. My original plans were diminishing as the minutes passed. I would arrive with barely enough time to visit one friend, let alone the various families I had hoped to call on. At this point I still believed that I would reach Tver, and the train seemed to be setting a fair pace after many hours of crawling along or making unscheduled halts. I reasoned that there must be several more northbound trains crawling from one siding to the next, as the southbound express trains took priority over the many single sections of track. Important officials clearly don't travel by *Electreechka*, or we might have received preferential treatment. But when your train's most important passenger is the babushka who walks through the carriages selling beer, mineral water, pasties, sweets and magazines, I guess you have to be thankful that at least you won't starve as you're shunted into yet another siding.

While the word *babushka* translates as grandmother, it is generally applied to any and all old women of a certain disposition. I had often enjoyed the company of such women during my travels in Russia, and smiled as I recalled one particular conversation from earlier that year. It had been a cold and snowy day in early March when I'd made the trip from Tver to Moscow by train, feeling a little uneasy in the unusually quiet carriages. Alighting in Moscow and boarding the Metro to the University where I had a meeting with a tutor, I couldn't help but wonder what had happened. Fair enough, it was the weekend, but that had never affected the transport systems or the streets so noticeably. Where was everyone?

Entering the university building my footsteps echoed on the concrete stairs, disturbing no-one but the stray cats. It was my first time in the building, and I'd walked several corridors and flights of stairs calling out, *'Privyet!'* – 'Hello!' – but there wasn't a soul around. I'd lived in Russia for long enough to know that times for meetings were often approximate but I had a train to catch back to Tver that day, so I raised my voice.

At long last a familiar face greeted me. I had first met this man back in the UK at the University of Leeds and he had invited me to study at Moscow State University. I was glad to see him, but had to ask about the deserted city. What was going on? When he explained about the date, it all became crystal clear. It was International Women's Day, the eighth of March. How could I forget? It was a national holiday and, when women take the day off in Russia, the entire country grinds to a halt. It was a wonder I'd managed to make the journey at all.

He apologised for the poor reception I'd had but rapidly made up for this when he invited me to join him and other staff in a room nearby. I entered this room to discover a long table practically groaning with food and drinks and surrounded by many university staff, almost all of whom were female. As the occasion demanded, I took my place and raised my rapidly filled glass in a toast.

'Sisterhood!'

The party continued and I quickly discussed the details of my studies before I lost the ability to talk sense. One tutor, Elena, sat at the far end of the table from me, called to me about my current lodgings. Where was I living in Tver? Perhaps in a student hostel? My reply, in Russian, was an often-repeated one.

'No, I live with a typical Russian babushka.'

This woman wanted more information and asked, *'Shto znachit – typeechnaya Ruskaya babushka?'* – 'What do you mean by a typical Russian babushka?'

My answer, again in Russian, poured forth as easily as the vodka.

'Well, you know, she offers a better exchange rate than the banks.'

The men were seriously outnumbered and smiled politely as the women roared with laughter. If I'd felt awkward, I needn't have done. I was one of them now.

Many a true word is spoken in jest, so the saying goes, but my joke bore the hallmarks of reality in the newly emerging market economy that Russia was struggling to come to terms with. Time after time I found it was women who had grasped the nettle and adjusted far better to the strange new world following the collapse of the Soviet Union. They not only drove the buses, trams, trolley buses and even trains; they practically drove the economy forward. Whether sat on a stool knitting socks made from woven dog hair in minus twenty degrees of frost, or patrolling the carriages of trains selling food, drinks, magazines and batteries to passengers, these women made a lasting impression. As for my joke, well it was true. They did offer better exchange rates, eager to buy hard currencies while the rouble ploughed a difficult furrow.

My train felt like it was ploughing rock by this point: stop, start, stop start. The many unscheduled pauses were not without merit but only if you were brave enough to avail yourself of the natural facilities, namely the birch trees. I noticed many male passengers alighting at these times. The women had greater self-control and dignity, or was it simply the height of the climb to re-board the train from track level that persuaded them to tolerate any discomfort? Nevertheless, I watched the men with increasing envy the longer our journey took.

Shortly after two o'clock the train pulled in to another nameless station, or rather more of a sparse platform offering a couple of roughly hewn seats, whereupon all the remaining passengers disembarked. I was rather more indignant than worried when I found myself, once again, the sole occupant of the train. Standing in the corridor beside the open carriage door, my mind was in turmoil. Should I get off and risk being stranded in this rural retreat, surrounded by birch trees as far as the eye could see? I knew I could desperately use a birch tree by this time but had no desire to spend the night under one. The platform was bare – no signs, maps, ticket office or evidence of human habitation. Where was I, and how could I return to civilisation?

After ten minutes or so a few new passengers began arriving and boarding the train. I plucked up the courage to ask someone which station this was, choosing a young woman carrying a baby as a likely source of reliable information. That was before her *friends* arrived – a group of gypsies, whose dark skins almost certainly confirmed their Georgian origins. Realising I was lost and foreign, one of them kept insisting I give her money and she would tell me all I wanted to know. Naturally I refused, inviting them to pass by and enter the carriage. However, their ruse was well-practised for no-one else would attempt to pass them as long as they obstructed the door, so the carriage behind me remained empty, while I remained surrounded by these vultures.

Foolishly I handed over a few coins, no more than fifty pence worth of roubles, and the spokeswoman dutifully informed me that Tver was three stops further. I thanked her and turned to go back into the carriage, noticing how a few passengers had finally entered it via another door. But these gypsies know rich pickings when they see them, and another one of their clan grabbed my hand and tried to tell me my fortune, which from where I was standing did not look particularly rosy at the time. She also insisted on payment for her services, so I pretended not to understand. She kept on insisting. I kept refusing. After a minute or so I forced my way brusquely through the pack and wrenched open the sliding door to the main carriage. The fortune-teller swore and roughly grabbed hold of my thin jacket and hair, and I responded likewise, pulling away roughly and also swearing. After a year in Russia, particularly when customs had seized my laptop computer at Sheremyetovo Airport in Moscow, I'd had ample opportunity to get to grips with the vernacular. I took a seat beside some amiable looking Russian women, and when the gypsies followed me into the carriage they accepted their defeat and my gesture that they should walk on by.

I had serious reservations over Tver being three stops further on and my doubts were soon verified when the train set off and began heading back the way it had just come. Three stops brought us back to a station I had already visited once – Reshenikovo. By this time I knew I would have to answer nature's call very soon. The bottle of mineral water I had consumed several hours earlier had long-since added to my discomfort. There was no way I could endure the journey all the way back to Moscow, for I was certain that after five hours of random journeying the train had to be heading back to Moscow. This also meant that I now had an invalid ticket and so, with no desire to fall foul of Russian bureaucracy, once we pulled in at Klin, I got off.

Klin was not unknown to me. This is where Tchaikovsky spent many happy years and I'd visited the beautiful house-museum on two separate occasions. Unfortunately the public conveniences were not as easy to locate, but ten frustrating minutes later came my blessed relief. These facilities mirrored the design at Moscow's Lenningradski Vauxhal, in that there were no toilets as such, more a hole in the tiled floor. Even this could not spoil my sincere gratitude to the attendant for remaining at her post on such a delightfully sunny day.

Next came the decision to end all decisions. Should I go north to Tver, or south to Moscow, and home? Klin is midway between these two cities, but based on my experiences of the day I decided to take the safer option and go home. I approached the ticket office and bought a one-way ticket to Moscow, before asking several people which platform this train departed from. As I waited I calculated the day's expenses and arrived at a figure of almost fifty roubles, which was about eight pounds sterling then. This was the fee for a day spent sightseeing, with the sights restricted almost exclusively to birch trees. Considering that I could see nothing *but* birch trees from my roost in Krasnogorsk on Moscow's northern flank, I reckoned I should have spent the day on the balcony at home.

My inner detective managed to discover where I went wrong. It turned out there was a separate branch line near Tver, and while I originally boarded a train for Tver, I was then obliged to change trains with no warning. The replacement train, instead of taking the main line, took this obscure little branch line. In order to reach Tver it was necessary for me to change trains at a tiny station called ... wait for it ... Reshenikovo! So the gypsy hadn't been lying after all but nor was she going to elaborate on the details for a mere fifty pence. That was for her to know and me to find out about.

Over the next few days I drew upon this experience more and more, and still do many years later. That train journey reflected all that was wrong with the Soviet ideal. I boarded a train, confident that I would reach my destination, assured that the train would take me there. I then endured sheer hell as I was pushed around, confused, lied to and left fending for myself, before returning back to where I'd started without ever having reached the promised destination. I even had to suffer financial loss and risk physical injury for the privilege.

And yet these people had put up with this every single day for seventy long years. Since then the country has undergone radical change and many lament the losses. They *still* sit on that Soviet train, their heads bloodied and bandaged, threatened by vagabonds and completely at the mercy of an unseen force. Nevertheless, they rarely complain and their faith in the promised destination endures.

In recent times whenever Russia enters our homes, it's inevitably politics and conflict that we hear about. Some of us may think Russia has ridden this particular train too far, pursuing a line that doesn't exist with a now invalid ticket. But 'Russia' is so much more than the leaders often condemned in the news – like every nation on the planet, it is individuals who constitute society. You don't need to look far to observe this. Any bus, tram, train or plane journey gives us the chance to see beyond the headlines and accusations. The people occupying seats close-by are not that different. We can all ride the same vehicle, carrying our own baggage, our own beliefs. Motives, status, conscience and desire will influence our choices, and it's perfectly possible for two travellers to share the same carriage when their destinations lie in opposite directions. A Russian once told me, 'Truth is what works for you', and here lies that possibility. One traveller may disembark sooner, while the other will need patience, tolerance, courage, and perhaps a little luck.

Following the unexpected Brexit vote in the UK, who knows what these passengers will do? Maybe Scotland will disembark sooner and choose to board a European express, while others will stay on course for whatever destination awaits them, be that a nameless station on a rarely used branch line or a major urban interchange.

That sign at the end of the platform greeted me again upon my return to Moscow – the one that read *'Vezdyeh'* – 'Everywhere'. Still it speaks volumes about Russia's recent history, and how their journey to 'everywhere' became a fruitless one to nowhere in particular. These down-trodden passengers found themselves right back where they started – but do they give up? Do they hell!

'Never mind,' they say. *'Kak nam tyazhelo.'* – 'Life's tough.'

So they try again the next day, and the next. Had the Soviet leaders acknowledged and respected the strength of human faith and its ability to overcome all obstacles, the result may have been very different. Clearly they missed a vital point that we'd all do well to heed. It really isn't the destination that matters. What's important is how we cope with the journey.

VALERIE HORTON

After a twenty-year career in IT, Valerie Horton decided to dedicate more time to the creative side of life. With a degree in English Language and Literature and a Diploma in Creative Writing, from the Open University, she has continued to develop her craft, completing a number of short stories specialising in tales with a twist. Her children's poems were received well at the Edinburgh Festival in 2001, and she has re-edited a children's book she wrote some years ago, with a view to publication. Currently, she is in the final stages of editing a speculative fiction novel.

Valerie has travelled throughout Europe and Scandinavia, visiting over twenty countries, for both work and pleasure. She taught English to teenagers and adults in the south of Poland for a year and is currently exploring the use of writing as a therapy for those who have experienced trauma.

Along with creative writing, Valerie has a passion for music – playing a number of musical instruments including piano, guitar, tenor horn and flute. She has played in public with a number of brass and concert bands.

Valerie lives in her home county of Yorkshire, and aspires to be a successful writer, spreading enjoyment via the written word.

COMMENDED
OUEN PRESS
SHORT STORY COMPETITION 2016

INTO THE BLUE
by Valerie Horton

'Empty your pockets,' she demanded.

Money, keys, shopping lists, old receipts, spilled on to the counter.

'Jewellery?' she asked, scrutinising my neck and ears.

I pointed to my watch and raised my eyebrows. She nodded, as I placed my watch alongside my other belongings. She pointed to the white bathroom scales just to my left. Feeling unstable, due to an acute attack of nerves, I stepped onto them with care. She recorded my weight on the ticket she gave me, before directing me to a door diagonally opposite the one through which I had entered the small shed-like cabin. Framed in the doorway, I stood holding on to both sides for support, ticket in hand, looking at what was to come.

My mouth was dry. My heart screamed to escape. Part of me wanted to run away, leave immediately. Part of me feared what was to come. Part of me was excited by the prospect. I stepped through the door to the other side, onto a landing, above an area of grass cordoned off by temporary fencing. Self-conscious, I looked at the crowds around the perimeter, relaxing a little when I realised they weren't watching me. All eyes were focused on the next incumbent of the position I would soon be taking up myself. Holding onto the rail, I walked down the steps slowly and with care.

There were four hard, plastic seats within the cordon, three close together, side-by-side. The other was on the same latitude but a little distance away. A fifth seat, the hot seat, a wooden kitchen chair, was placed almost centrally within the arena. An arena surrounded by crowds of onlookers, three or four people deep, all eager for spectacle. I imagined it to be similar to a public hanging back in the 17- or 1800s. A crowd baying for blood. Hoping for, cheering for, the worst to happen – to someone else, not them. Inwardly I smirked at the idea of what was about to happen. It was not far off that hanging scenario, and it was going to happen to me.

I looked at the occupants of the three chairs close to me. Were those smiles on their faces, or grimaces? Were their nerves as ragged as mine? Did they feel the same mixture of fear and excited anticipation as I did? Had they been able to eat any breakfast that morning? I hadn't.

I made my way to the desk just to my right. Again, I stepped onto a set of bathroom scales, as requested. This weight almost matching that written on my ticket, I was given a sickly green tabard to wear – as if I didn't feel ill enough. I was led to the first, now vacant chair, where I sat, grateful for the support, as my nerves bounced around, like a ball in a pinball machine.

My eyes flitted around the arena. At the crowds. At what was to come. My friends. Where were my friends? I couldn't see them in the crowd. But I knew they must be there, somewhere. But right now I had more important things to focus on. An attendant knelt down in front of me before binding my ankles together. He told me to put my feet closer together, so he could bind them tighter. He bound them so tightly, there was no give at all. It was impossible to separate one foot from the other. Impossible even to fit a finger between them. I felt totally immobilised. And to think I'd volunteered for this. Paid even.

The only way to travel when trussed up like a chicken, is to bunny hop. Thus I travelled to the next seat, which had just become vacant, as each of the other chickens had moved along one. Another would-be chicken joined us, to my right. Was that a smile, or a grimace she was giving me? What did she make of the smile/grimace I returned?

As I sat, my mind whirling with excitement, adrenalin and not a little anxiety, a stranger stooped before me, checking my bonds. He pulled on them hard, ensuring they were secure. Ensuring there was no chance of escape. No chance of backing out. Appearing satisfied, he looked up, smiling his evident knowledge of what in store for me, as I hopped to the next seat along. Another chicken joined us, to our right.

Eventually, I made it to the fourth seat, the one on the same line, but set apart from the others. A different stranger looked at my ticket, checked the colour of the tabard I was wearing and, like the previous strangers, checked the security of my ankle bonds. As satisfied as the previous strangers had been, he indicated for me to go and sit in the vacant chair in the middle of the arena. The hot seat.

It is impossible to bunny hop with dignity. Having to do so, for several hops, in front of a watchful crowd, made it all the more difficult. That, coupled with knowing what was to come – or rather, not knowing *exactly* what was to come, made the journey to the centre of the arena interminably long.

The further I hopped, the more unstable I became. Nervous tension made my legs shake, wobble, to the point of near collapse. I stretched my arms forward to clutch the back of the kitchen chair, for essential support. Hopping round to the front, my legs straining, I fell sideways into the chair, with a huge exhalation, relieved to have reached the seat before my legs buckled completely. It was only from the safety of the hot seat, that I realised the eyes of the crowd had not been on me at all. They'd all been watching the chicken in front of me, as he'd been whisked away in a metal cage.

A final strange man knelt before me, holding the end of what looked like a long, thick, white rope. Once again he checked my bonds, tugging them sharply against my ankles, almost pulling me off the shiny chair seat. He nodded his satisfaction, before comparing the coloured end of the rope, with that of the tabard I was wearing. A perfect, sickly match.

The cage that had whisked away the trussed up chicken in front of me, returned, empty. A trembling surge flooded my body, immersing each muscle in complete impotence. It was pure bravado that gave me the strength to complete my final set of bunny-hops, taking me to the yellow cage, where I was greeted by a kindly-looking older man with greying hair and a warm smile, who helped me as I half-jumped, half-pulled myself into the metal crate. Once inside, I was relieved to see a small, triangular, metal seat across the back right hand corner of the cage. Using both man and metal for support, I made it to the seat, flopping into it, thinking – *I've made it.*

The cage began to rise, yet my anxiety lessened as the kindly man closed the gate through which I'd entered. I relaxed convincing myself – *The gate's closed. I'm safe.* As we ascended, the gatekeeper instructed me on what to do once we reached the top.

'It does nothing for you,' he added. 'But it looks more impressive for the crowd.'

I told him not to push me. I assured him I would do what was required, but I definitely did not want pushing into it. I recalled what had happened to one I'd seen earlier. One who'd hesitated. One who appeared to have been pushed. But he'd clung on. With one hand still grasping the metal, he'd crashed into the side of the cage. He'd called out, shouted and scrabbled in equal measure. The kindly man had had to haul him back before returning him to the ground. As the scrabbler had exited the arena he'd looked pale, wan, had insipid skin, and such wide, vacant eyes, with grey bags beneath – he'd barely looked alive.

Back in the still rising cage, the kindly man assured me he would not push me into doing anything. The cage stopped. 170 feet above ground.

'The same height as the Hilton Hotel in Leeds', the man informed me.

I can't say that was a kindly act. He then performed another unkindly act. He opened the gate. Internally, I screamed. *No!* I'd lost my sense of security. While the gate had been closed, I'd felt safe, secure. But now…

The man offered to help me, but I declined preferring to hold onto reliable, solid metal. I shuffled close to the edge. As close as my comfort zone would allow.

'Move further forward,' the man said.

I moved further forward – a fraction of an inch.

'Closer,' he said again, 'so your toes are over the lip of the cage.'

Was he mad? Did he not realise there was a 170 foot drop in front of me? I gripped the top of the cage, either side of the gate, whilst manoeuvring into position.

I gripped tightly, yet the once-kindly man worked my thumbs loose – those opposing digits, developed over millennia to aid us with our gripping – and he was loosening them.

'So they don't become dislocated, or worse,' he told me.

His tone was reassuring. I found the words disturbing.

I stood on the brink, toes over the lip of the cage, hands gripping the metal so hard with my fingers to compensate for lack thumbs, that my knuckles looked to be covered in rice-paper.

'Don't look down,' the sometimes-kindly man advised. 'If you look down, you won't do it. Just look at the horizon.'

I looked. I looked hard. I gazed at the peaceful blue sky stretching all the way into the far distance. I saw green fields spotted with indiscernible animals. I saw a roof-scape that would have made an excellent jigsaw puzzle. Over to my far left I could see hills of various hues – purple, brown and yellow – as the sunshine and shadows danced around each other. The heat of the sun on my face felt a deep, contented warm.

The tranquil view is what I stared at, but what I focused on was the voice of the once-kindly man, steeling myself for that one particular word. As with the trussed up chickens before me, the man stretched his right arm over and out the side of the cage, shouting, loud enough for the spectators below to hear.

'Three!' He yelled, displaying that number of fingers.

I focused on what I would do when I heard *the* word.

'Two!' He shouted, displaying two fingers, laterally.

When he says it, I do it, I thought. That's all I could think.

'One!'

One finger. It's getting close. He's going to say it. Any time now. When he says it, I…

'Bungee!'

Without hesitation I leapt from the cage, pushing against the metal as hard as my weak legs were able, to clear the crate. My fingers released from the cage, my thumbs coming with them, un-dislocated. I leapt into the tranquil blue, stretching out my arms into the crowd-impressing swan dive.

I was free. Flying. Exhilarated. For the first time, I experienced the feeling of not touching anything. The restraints around my ankles exerted no pressure. I had no weight against the ground. Just air, all around me. Total lack of restriction. Total liberation. An intense sense of release. Flying free like…

The horizon disappeared. The calming blue disappeared. The floating freedom disappeared. Rooftops appeared, rising at an alarming rate. Not wishing to see the hard structure of houses rushing towards me, I looked towards the ground. I saw grass, and people, ascending at the same disturbing pace. I was powerless to stop them. Relentlessly they rushed towards me. I began to feel great pressure on my eyes. In a bid to protect them, I shut my eyelids.

Another sensation surged through me. Falling. Fast, yet blindly. Not knowing how far from the ground I was. Not knowing when the tug of the bungee rope would pull. Not knowing *if* the tug of the bungee rope would pull. I seemed to have been falling much more than 170 feet. Much more than the few seconds it had taken the others to descend.

Shouldn't the rope have kicked in by now? Was the rope secure? Would it work? Would it hold? Shouldn't it have stopped my descent by now? Shouldn't I now be rising skyward again? All thoughts of the repeated, meticulous, safety checks had flown my mind. All that remained was hope – or prayer.

Not before time, I felt the welcome tug of the bungee rope. Despite this, however, I continued to descend. I was relieved to know the rope had worked, had held. The continuing descent lasted less than a second, before I felt myself rising, upside down, happy in the knowledge the rope was secure.

Ecstatic, my rise continued. I opened my eyes to relish the experience to its fullest extent. I saw trees twist and turn around me, before dissolving into sky. Clouds appeared like watchful angels. The tranquil blue returned.

I saw a loop of rope drop below me. A loop created as the rope descended, yet I continued upwards. My feet reached the zenith of the rise, yet my body continued skyward. My shoulders passed my feet as the latter halted yet the former continued to rise. For a second or two, I was standing in mid air. Standing on nothing. Like a magician, I was levitating above the ground, stared at in awe by the crowds below. I twisted on the spot, spinning and turning like a demented Dervish before toppling sideways, feeling a sharp wrench in the middle of my back. Once again, I was descending, but this time the ground was rushing towards me at a most peculiar angle.

All these sensations were repeated two or three times. Each iteration to a lesser extent than the previous one. I heard voices, distant, yet distinct. It was only now that I realised how silent everything had been. Had there been any noise from the crowd? With previous jumpers I'd heard cheers and applause. Or had I been so caught up in the world of bungee, I'd been deaf to the world of spectators?

'Hold your arms up,' repeated the voice.

I did so, yet I was disoriented, confused. I raised my arms skyward, in the usual manner, yet felt them alongside my body.

'Hands down. Hold your hands down.'

I am holding them down, I thought. I can feel them against me. Realisation seeped in. I was in an upside down world. I reversed the position of my arms. Hands grabbed each of my wrists. My shoulders complained as I was hauled sideways towards the landing strip – a thin mattress, on which I was laid down. I looked towards the centre of the arena and saw a large, blue, inflated mattress. Where had that been when I'd needed it?

Someone fumbled at my feet. I felt release of the bonds I hadn't noticed since entering the cage. I lay on the thin mattress feeling a heady mixture of exhilaration, excitement, exhaustion – and relief. I wanted to lie there relaxing, soaking up the entire experience while I recovered, but was interrupted by the instruction.

'OK, you can get up now.'

But, I want to stay – I thought, unable yet to speak. I want to savour the experience. Relish the utter relaxation after such exhilarating stress.

'You must get up now,' the unkind voice said again.

Must. I must get up. So much for relaxation.

'You can collect your things at the desk.'

I struggled to my feet, holding onto the owner of the voice for support.

'Don't forget to pick up your things on your way out. The desk is just there.'

She pointed, but I barely took notice. All I could think was – *they expect me to walk?* To walk on legs devoid of substance, devoid of muscle, devoid of strength.

If I'd thought my bunny hops had been ungainly, my gait immediately after my bungee jump was worse than that of a drunkard. However, the ground itself seemed to give me the strength I needed, along with the cheers and applause of friends in the crowd, who'd endured – enjoyed? the same experience earlier in the day. I held on to the temporary fencing and stared at the desk, which inched closer, seemingly of its own accord. My head danced in ever-increasing circles, as my dizziness abated, and my erratic, shortened breathing became longer and smoother.

I reached the desk where I was given back my possessions, and released back out into the community – as a responsible member of society.

The experience within the arena did not stay within the arena. It stayed with me. If I could bunny hop in front of crowds, and survive; if I could do a bungee jump, and relish the experience; if I could face the fear of the unknown, and come out the other side, I could do anything; face any anything; cope with anything.

The feeling of pure exhilaration continued for weeks. I felt light, free, walking on air. Nothing troubled me. Traffic jams on the way to work, no longer mattered, as I recalled the freedom of the jump. Previously insurmountable problems, I could soar above. Congratulations from colleagues lifted me higher. I could now see that my boss, who wanted to control me – bully me, even – couldn't. I was free to remember the liberation, the exhilaration and the excitement of the jump. I was free to live as I wanted, and not be subject to the unjust demands of others. I was free to choose what I wanted. I was free to do the job I wanted. I was free to leave the job hated. I was free.

ROBBIE GILMORE

Robbie Gilmore is a sailor, adventurer, and expert croquet tactician. Growing up on the shores of Strangford Lough, Northern Ireland, he was introduced to the water at a young age. More often found camping on islands than in his own bed, Robbie soon developed a love for the great outdoors and a passion for sailing.

During his teenage years, he began to sail competitively, winning the Irish Youth championships and representing Ireland on the international stage.

A place at Cambridge University nearly left him landlocked, and meant the displeasure of having to squeeze lectures around a busy sailing and rowing schedule. However, it also unearthed an interest in writing which increasingly became entwined with his various water-based adventures around the globe. Long summer holidays provided plenty of time for travelling. Highlights included working for an NGO in Tanzania, coaching in upstate New York, and an impromptu canoeing trip down the Hudson River.

On Graduating, Robbie took the long route home, cycling from Cambridge to Spain before heading back to Ireland. Since then, Robbie has decided to take his sailing to the next level. Currently competing in the Olympic 49er class, he aims to represent Ireland at the 2020 Olympic Games. When not training or competing he spends his time writing about his adventures and experiences.

COMMENDED
OUEN PRESS
SHORT STORY COMPETITION 2016

CANOEING ON THE HUDSON
AN UNCONVENTIONAL AIRPORT TRANSFER
by Robbie Gilmore

The inspiration for our voyage came from decidedly modest roots. One August morning Rob and I lay sulking in our living room. There were several reasons for our foul moods. Firstly, we were hungover. We had been at a sorority party the night before, which had come to a stunning conclusion when Rob had thrown up all over the beer-pong table. An evening we would rather forget. Secondly, and directly linked to this, we had no breakfast in the house. At this point in time, the trek to the nearest supermarket seemed like it would be an epic, impossible journey. Finally, and most significantly, we were both contemplating the fact that we would soon have to leave America and return to Ireland in time for college to start again. The two of us had been working as sailing instructors in Ithaca, upstate New York for the whole summer and the idea of sitting in a damp lecture theatre, listening to a professor drone on about some obscure theory seemed decidedly less exciting than the heady buzz of a New York summer.

As Rob lay and moaned on the opposite couch, I opened up my laptop to have a look at the map. I knew that planning the trip to the airport sooner rather than later would probably be sensible. To get back to Newark airport for our flights we would have to take the greyhound bus to Albany and then down to New York City. But as my hungover eyes squinted at the screen, trying to pick out the route, a thin blue line caught my attention – the Hudson River.

In hindsight I must have still been a little drunk, because before I knew what was happening I had asked Rob the most ridiculous question.

'Hey Rob, the Hudson goes from Albany to

New York. Why don't we canoe down it?'

I felt like I was standing in a bar, and had just told a stranger that I loved her. The words had been conjured up inside me and left my lips before my brain had time intervene. Rob was obviously looking for something to distract him from the pain of the previous night. Before I knew what was happening he had jumped out of his chair and yelled –

'YES JOHN! Let's do it!'

It was as if that stranger in the bar had just grabbed me by the neck and landed a big kiss square on my lips. I was completely aware that I didn't know what I was doing, but it was great fun, and I was just going to close my eyes and hope for the best.

For the next three weeks we didn't bother looking at the map again. We were far too excited, telling anyone who would lend a sympathetic ear about our wild plans. It would be no small undertaking. The Hudson is one of the largest rivers in North America, over three miles wide at points, and we would have to paddle over 200 kilometres in five days to get to New York City to catch our flights home. The key to our success would be preparation.

These realities were rather lost on us. The

whole plan was a great story to tell sorority girls at parties, not something we needed to really prepare for. This bubble burst suddenly when three days before departure we realised that we didn't have a canoe. Rob and I sat down either side of the kitchen table and took a long, sober look at each other.

'John. Are we really going to do this thing?' Rob asked me.

'I don't know Rob. Can we?'

'I think we have to mate,' Rob responded, with a note of concern in his voice.

'Absolutely,' I replied.

We just had to do it. Why? Well firstly we had basically told the whole of Cornell University[1] about our plans. We knew that we might never be back here, but we couldn't face the prospect of having to inform all our new-found friends that we had chickened out. Least of all the sorority girls. They would not be impressed. Secondly, the more people told us that it was impossible, the more we wanted to do it. It was something truly exceptional, which the locals deemed impossible. Perhaps we were crazy, or perhaps our outsider's

[1] Cornell University basically encompasses the whole of Ithaca town. Most of our friends (including the sorority girls) were linked to the university in some way.

perspective gave us a different outlook on the whole thing. But we just felt that we had to prove to them, and ourselves, that it was possible. Overall, it felt like this idea had landed in my head almost by accident, and it would be a total waste to disregard it. Never in our lives would we be in a position to undertake this trip ever again. If we didn't do it now, it would never happen.

We pulled out our laptops and set to work. Soon we had found a canoe on Craigslist, and made a frighteningly long list of *'essential equipment'*. The next three days passed in a blur. We cycled manically around town, searching for all the gear we would need to make the trip: camping stoves, tarpaulins, hammocks and rations. Every time we got to the shop checkout we caught each other's eyes. Both of us knew we had the same thought going around our heads – *are we really doing this?* But neither of us wanted to be the one to say it out loud.

The day before our departure, our canoe arrived. It was the perfect vessel for such an adventure, a sturdy sixteen foot aluminium Grumman. It was big enough to carry all of our gear, and heavy enough that our lack of paddling experience hopefully wouldn't present too much of a problem. We went for a practice lap of the dock. After a close call with a motorboat and a near capsize we decided that practice was overrated, and pulled the canoe out of the water to store her for the night.

I hadn't been nervous until that night. Initially I hadn't thought about the trip as much more than a crazy idea, and by the time it had started to become a reality, I hadn't had the time to think about it too much. Now, lying in my bed for the last night, my brain began to spin nervously through every possible hurdle we might face. I guess that is the reason most people don't do crazy trips like this. They think about all the barriers and let those dominate their perspective, instead of truly exploring the idea and trying to bring it to reality. Fortunately for me, a coincidental combination of alcohol, pride, hectic schedule and youthful naivety had prevented me from thinking about these issues before this point. By now the canoe was lying in our front garden filled to the brim with essential kit, my alarm was set for six a.m., and I could already hear Rob snoring in the next room. It had all suddenly become real.

o0o

Day One

Our mate Chris gave us a lift from Ithaca down to the river. By nine we were crossing the Albany Bridge, where we were given our first sight of the challenge ahead. I stuck my head out the window, eager to get a better look, and nearly vomited down the side of the car. The river was enraged. White caps foamed upstream, carving the surface of the water into heaving trails of spume.

A fierce wind was blowing straight upstream and directly against our direction of travel, adding to the tide[2] which was also going to be opposing us for the next six hours. Despite my lack of experience, I had a bad feeling there was a tough day ahead, and deep down I feared we had totally underestimated the difficulty of the task in front of us.

Rob summed it up more succinctly

'Holy Shit!' he exclaimed beneath his breath, staring down at the river below.

Our first wobbling paddle-strokes were hardly inspirational. After nearly capsizing the

---

[2] Although we were over 200km upstream from the sea the tide still had a significant impact on the river flow. Like on the sea it turned every six hours, flowing downstream for six, and then back upstream for six. As such, it made a massive difference to our speed.

heavily-laden canoe just metres from the bank, we started meandering our way out into the stream. Paddling the canoe was tough. At first, balance and co-ordination were the main issue. It took time and concentration for us to get our strokes together, and every time the canoe wobbled we would smash our thumbs off the gunwale, slicing them open on the coarse metal. But soon other problems faced us. Blisters for one, and aching heavy shoulders. The continual buffeting of the wind made paddling heavy and difficult. It gusted unpredictably through the trees and whipped up an aggressive chop.

It was one of those windy blue-skied days, where the only clouds you can see are mere smears on the atmosphere, skidding along high in the Jetstream. Such days make everything seem brighter and more colourful. I imagined someone standing on one of those clouds looking down at us. A tiny grey speck in a sea of blue and white smudges, walled in on either side by the pulsing canopy of dark-green trees.

At water level, the picture was altogether less romantic. The hot sun and harsh wind felt like they were ripping at my skin. Every time it felt like we were getting a rhythm we smashed our way into a wave, bringing the canoe to a halt, and forcing us to start all over again. But we drove on, dipping and driving our paddles in a punchy rhythm, gritting our teeth, and revelling in the challenge.

There was something beautiful about the simplicity of our situation. For the first time in months I had nothing to think about, except the challenge in front of me. There were no questions or worries, no concerns or fears in my mind. All I had to do was take one stroke after another, battle the river, and keep moving forwards.

We paddled all day, only pulling in as the sun began to dip over the western bank. Pulling out our phones – our only means of navigation – we checked our progress, and nearly cried. Eleven kilometres completed, 190 to go. At this rate of travel I wouldn't have a whole lot of time shopping in duty free at the airport.

Mulling this over, I fired up the stove and examined our rations. Tins were our main provision, as they would survive best sloshing around in the bottom of a canoe for four days. Picking up some Wal-Mart chilli con carne, I realised we had made a disastrous error.

'Rob, where the hell is the tin opener?'

'Ahhh… Come here you fecker. Watch this.'

Rob flicked open some hidden implement on his penknife and began to work on the tin. Within twenty seconds he levered it open – crisis averted. As we sat and watched the beans bubble I reflected on how lucky I was to have such an excellent companion. Rob was a Scout Leader, in the Army Reserves, and an avid Gaelic football player, giving him both a great deal of outdoor experience and an excellent level of fitness.

However, he was also hard as nails, and possibly slightly mad. At that moment we had a serious difference of opinion about how to deal with our lack of progress. I thought that the best solution was to have a good meal, hang our hammocks and get some decent rest. That way we would be ready to push on hard tomorrow and make up for our lack of mileage. Rob wasn't convinced. He was all set to power on into the darkness. The tide was turning and the wind was dropping, which would definitely help us to travel a bit quicker.

But, there were a couple of problems with this idea. Firstly, we didn't have a map, or a clue what lay ahead of us. A collision with a bridge, in a canoe, with no buoyancy, wouldn't be an ideal situation in the pitch black. Secondly, if one of us went overboard, the chances of picking up the body – dead or alive – would be pretty slim. At this point the river was nearly half a mile wide, and our only lights were two Wal-Mart head-torches, which aren't quite up to search-and-rescue standards. Finally, we had seen several ships going up and down the river, and they were huge. In the darkness they would have no chance of seeing us. If they hit us, they would feel about as much as a truck crushing a pencil. While we would be sucked underneath their hulls and shredded by their spinning propellers.

Despite this, after wrapping up the stove, Rob managed to convince me to step back into the canoe. This was partly because he had cooked me dinner, for which I was incredibly grateful, but also because I knew in my gut that we just had to make more progress.

After paddling for a while I congratulated him on his good judgement. The conditions and our rhythm were getting better all the time, helping the canoe to pulse downstream. The tide was now really with us. Something we had not anticipated would be so important when we had planned the trip. We resolved to work in shifts from now on, only paddling when the tide was with us so we didn't tire ourselves out. We both fell into silence, thinking about the river in front of us. I listened to the wind rushing in the trees on the banks, the swilling of our paddles through the water, and the occasional gurgling crash of the bows through a wave.

At around eleven p.m. the lights from Hudson town passed by on the western bank. Stealing quietly past civilisation, and paddling on confidently into the blackness ahead, I felt like the adventure was truly beginning. We had really broken away from normality. While the rest of the world sat in their living rooms and watched the ten o'clock news, here we were sweating in the blackness, voyaging silently on into the night.

I was soon to learn why most people choose to spend their time in such mundane settings. Ahead of us the blackness was cut by a lightning bolt, striking down over the Catskill Mountains. The thunder rolled over the valley. A storm was brewing. No light prospect in a small canoe.

Within minutes the wind was building, and with it the waves. I was sitting in the bow, and subject to their full force. These weren't the round rushing waves of the day. These were steep black walls coming straight at me out of the dark. Spray flew all around me, spectral and white in the light of my head torch. All my philosophical pleasure in our situation quickly went out the window.

'Rob. This is nuts. Let's get ashore!' I shouted over the wind.

Rob wasn't convinced, but after a couple of waves swamped clean over the bow, he decided it was time to call it a night.

An hour later the rain began to drum on the hull of the canoe, inches from my nose. We had pulled in at a wooden jetty on the eastern shore, and after carrying the canoe to a soft-ish looking piece of grass, we had rolled her over to make a rudimentary shelter for the night. There isn't a whole lot of room under a canoe for two young men, and all the supplies they need for an expedition. I found myself wedged between several tins of peaches and Rob's feet. Soon he was snoring so loudly that I imagined I could hear the rivets holding the canoe together vibrating. I don't think the arrangement would be recommended in a modern-day sleep-clinic. Regardless, within a couple of minutes I was fast asleep.

The river had taught us a lesson today – respecting its power was going to be crucial for our survival, and we were very glad to be back on land safe, and with some better progress under our belts.

oOo

Day Two

The alarm went off at five a.m. – I felt like someone had wedged an axe between my shoulder blades and rubbed some gravel in my eyes. Rolling out from under the canoe, I lay spread-eagled, face-down in the grass, the morning dew soaking into my skin.

We still had 160 kilometres to go.

Our sole contact that morning was with a local fisherman from Catskill.

'The water goin' be rough today,' he said as he puttered past in a ramshackle little boat.

'Thanks! We'll be grand!' we yelled in reply, ploughing downstream, stripped to the waist with wild grins from ear to ear.

We soon realised our naivety, and his wisdom. Today the wind had sculpted proper waves. Waves that could have come from the sea. Waves that formed walls across the river that we were forced to smash our way through.

The river grew throughout the morning, stretching wider and wider. Yesterday we had been paddling around tight bends, past wooded islands, and close to the shore. Now the river was a mile across, with long straits, and meanders that disappeared into a distant sunny haze. Seeing the river rolling out in front of us made me realise the enormity of the challenge ahead.

We hung on, battering our way downstream, one wave at a time. Call me crazy, but beneath the sweat, sunburn and spray I was having a great time. I was revelling in the simplicity of the physical challenge. I didn't have to think about anything but putting the paddle into the water and ripping it backwards. There was little fear or thought involved, just a brutal physical challenge.

By twelve o'clock the tide had started to turn against us, and we pulled in on the beach to rest up for a while. We pulled in at a little State Park that rolled down to the riverbank. It was the perfect spot. A sandy beach allowed us to easily pull the canoe out of the water, and there was a pagoda just inshore where we could hang our hammocks and catch a few hours of rest. But just as we were beginning to drift off we heard the sound of a car engine.

Sitting up, I watched as a grey pickup with blacked out windows bounced across the grass towards the pagoda. I looked at Rob, and we both rolled out of our hammocks, ready to greet this stranger. A thickset man stepped out, his forearms bulging tight against the stitching of his checked shirt. I couldn't really see his face between the bottom of his peaked cap and thick bushy beard. He turned his head and spat a thick lump of tobacco out of his mouth. Rob and I bristled. We had been told by our college friends back at Ithaca Yacht Club to be aware of the locals around here. Apparently they were mostly avid fans of the second amendment, and not too welcoming to strangers.

The man ahead looked up at us. His face looked like the river on a windy day – a million wrinkles creased around his eyes, like waves rushing across the surface. He smiled a wide tobacco-stained grin and extended a thick hand.

'Well hey guys. I'm AJ. Can I join you for a bit? We was just going to have our Labor Day barbecue here. Hope you don't mind do you?'

Shaking his hand felt like entering a small cave. Rob and I agreed immediately that there was no problem with him sharing the pagoda with us, and helped him unload the pickup as his wife and son emerged from the passenger doors.

AJ was a true gentleman. He cooked us the most delicious lunch of sausages and hamburgers, and regaled us with all sorts of wild tales about his life in the Catskill Mountains. After we had finished eating, he leaned closely towards me and Rob.

'Hey guys, I have a little weed in the back of the truck. If you guys want some you are welcome to it. We just can't smoke it in front of the big guy,' he gestured over towards his son.

Rob and I politely but firmly declined. Our paddling was already erratic enough. Instead we climbed into our hammocks and slept with full bellies for the next three hours, while AJ and his family watched over our gear.

When we woke up in the early evening and headed off, they waved to us from the sandy beach. Once we had rounded the next bend Rob turned around in the bows and grinned back at me.

'Was that a dream?' he asked me gesturing back towards the park

'Yeah, I think so,' I replied.

We paddled on into the evening. As nightfall drew in, the wind began to die and soon the river was eerily calm. The canoe glided on through the water, splitting it into little ripples that widened past our transom. Soon it was totally pitch-black, and we could see nothing beyond the pool of light cast by our Wal-Mart head-torches. Occasionally a freight train would come roaring up the bank, and we would see its light cutting behind the trees. This was our only navigational aid.

The canoe was slipping along well. Rob and I had finally found our rhythm, and the canoe sliced easily through the glassy water. Compared to the previous two days this was a doddle. Even so, five hours later we were beginning to wane. We had spent nearly twelve hours in the canoe today, and our bodies were seriously beginning to fatigue.

Luckily we soon saw a glimmering light reflecting off the river surface in the distance. Rob worked in tandem to turn the canoe towards it. As we neared, we realised that it was a light marking the end of a Yacht Club pier. This was less than ideal – these clubs were often private and would probably not be pleased to find two stinking, half-naked Irish men sprawled on their dock. But glancing back into the eerie darkness we knew we had few other options.

We walked cautiously up to the clubhouse. On one hand I wanted nothing less than to have to get back in that canoe and paddle on into the unknown darkness, to try and find somewhere else to sleep. Equally, I didn't want to be discovered by a discontented shotgun-toting club member and tossed out of my hammock in the middle of the night. On this basis, we decided we had better see if there was anyone around. By this stage we must have been quite a sight. Both of us were stripped to the waist, wearing nothing but faded bathing shorts. Our bodies were tanned a deep shade of brown, and encrusted with an assorted mix of river-water and dried sweat. Rob was sporting a healthy quantity of facial hair. Not the standard look for a Yacht Club. I pushed open the door and stepped inside. Across the room sat five locals, who looked at us, mouths agape.

'Well, who the fuck are you?' the overweight, florid man behind the bar broke the awkward silence…

Rob and I glanced at each other, and I dived in.

'I'm John, and this is Rob. We are from Ireland….and eh…. we are canoeing down the river from Albany to… New York City…'

'We pulled in hoping we could catch some rest,' Rob chimed in.

Silence.

'Well… Get over here and sit the hell down boys! You must be half dead!'

Ice-cold Budweisers materialised in our hands and a new sheen of grease adhered to our already filthy vests, as monstrous steak sandwiches were forced into our mouths. This was hospitality to the point of aggression. We tried our best to recount our story and mumble repeated thanks through mouths jammed with food, before we were marched to the showers. Scrubbing ourselves clean, we staggered back to our hammocks – clean, full, and completely and utterly spent.

oOo

<u>Day Three</u>

My eyelids grated open as I fumbled around the pockets of my hammock, trying to switch off my five a.m. alarm. The fatigue was beginning to bite hard. Someone had added a hot poker to the axe already wedged between my shoulders. But this pain evaporated when I saw the smoking morning mist, wafting off the river. The wind was gone, and the conditions looked perfect. When I dropped my paddle into the glass-smooth water and took that first cool stroke, the canoe slipped along with the lightest of touches. Finally.

I was in a state of groggy euphoria. My brain was stuck in an exhausted hole, but just about aware of the beautiful pleasure to be had in caressing the canoe through the smooth water. As the mist began to clear in front of our bows, the Poughkeepsie Bridge poked around the corner ahead. A train horn blew in the distance and I could hear its wheels chattering up the valley. I felt like some sort of explorer in frontier America.

Rob however, was not enjoying himself quite so much. As we rounded the corner, ready to swing under the bridge he turned to me, and delivered a terrifying sentence.

'John… my shoulders are killing me. I can't take another stroke.'

My grogginess, and euphoria, flashed away. I was surprised, shocked, angry. These were the best conditions of the trip, how could he not be able to take another stroke? We had to make progress! How could he not have looked after himself better? This was ridiculous…

But I knew my anger was illogical, and any argument, futile. One glance at Rob's face and I could see it. He was broken.

As I pulled the canoe out of the water, Rob sat on the bank. He looked deflated. Both of his arms lay at his sides and his shoulders were rounded, kind of like a child who has just been told his pocket money has been confiscated.

But the situation wasn't quite that humorous. He was so exhausted he couldn't lift his paddle off the ground.

We only had one type of medicine with us – food. Corned-beef hash. A portion for 8 people. Then oranges, protein bars, trail mix, m-and-m's, apples, water – a gallon between us – cereal bars, and a pot of very, very strong tea. I had to patch Rob back together. If he was broken, the trip finished. However, as the current ebbed downstream, time was draining away. We had progressed just half a kilometre, and we had a very long way to go. We had to get back in the canoe quickly or else we would have to forfeit the trip, get on the bus, and head for New York, as failures.

This, we would not do, and soon Rob stepped carefully back into the canoe, determined to continue.

By now the sun was beating down. It was the hottest recorded day that summer, and we were being fried. The tin of the canoe made an excellent mirror, focusing the sun towards our weak Irish skin. But with every drop of sweat falling off my brow, my morale, and the energy in my muscles seemed to return. The food was kicking in, and there was a deep satisfaction in the knowledge that we had been tested to our limits, and persevered. From now on though we would have to be much, much more conservative. Our pace had been completely unsustainable. We ached all over, were dehydrated, constipated, ferociously sunburned, sleep-deprived, and our hands were covered in cuts and blisters. In our arrogant sprint for the first 125 kilometres from Albany we had been able to suppress all of these problems. If we wanted to make the next seventy-five, to Manhattan, we would have to take a more sustainable approach. If the first two days had taught us the importance of the elements, we now had a new-found respect for our own physical limits.

We reached Chelsea Yacht Club at midday. A friend of ours had put us in touch with some members there, and as we pulled in at the jetty the commodore stood ready to greet us. His enthusiastic handshake was met with my wince, as he squeezed the raw blister-covered flesh of my palm. My etiquette didn't improve much, and within five minutes I lay asleep, face down on the front lawn.

Four hours later, Rob resurrected me for dinner. The weekly Yacht Club meal was being prepared, and it was massive. By the end of it we were surrounded by members, amazed by our seemingly bottomless stomachs. When at long last we were satisfied, we sat and relaxed on the veranda, watching the sun drop over the eastern bank. This felt like heaven, but soon we had to leave this oasis, and begin paddling. Again.

But when we did, we were in great spirits. The stop had been the perfect opportunity for our bodies to recover, and a light tailwind had begun to nuzzle at our backs, encouraging us downstream. A beautiful red sunset lit the Black Mountains in front of us, and the moon lifted through the horizon. At last it felt like the elements were relenting, and for the first time we were able to enjoy the natural beauty around us. We pulled in for the night at a deserted beach opposite Newbridge town. The moon lit the gravel in front of us as we paddled in.

Within thirty seconds of our keel grounding, the mosquitoes attacked me from all angles, pouring out of the sky. I beat the air frantically, trying to put my hammock up before I was eaten alive. Once tucked safely the final burst of adrenaline ebbed from my veins and I felt exhausted. Today had been a stressful day – between helping Rob down the river, trying to make conversation with the Yacht Club commodore, and being attacked by mosquitoes at the last minute just when we thought we were home and dry. The caress of the canvas hammock around my shoulders felt blissful, and in seconds I was asleep.

o0o

Day Four
I jumped out of my hammock, feverishly working to strike camp before the mosquitoes could tear into my skin again. I had been woken in the middle of the night by the sound of rushing water and, peeking over my hammock, saw the river rushing-by underneath me. In my haste to get under my mosquito net the previous night I had evidently hung my hammock over the riverbank, and when the tide had come in it had come up right underneath me. I was too tired to care, and fell back to sleep. Fortunately when I woke up, the tide was going out, and I stepped out onto dry land rather than into knee-deep water.

That morning we would be paddling through the Bear Mountain State Park, where the river narrows and winds through the mountain, channelling and concentrating its flow. We hoped this would push us along, allowing us to shoot through the mountains.

But within an hour of setting off, nature threw another hurdle in the way – fog. Thick, clammy, barrelling, banks of it, rolling upstream towards us. Occasionally we would be given a tantalising glimpse of the bank, but otherwise we were lost. Every time I heard the horn of a freight train, I imagined a ship ploughing out of the white wall in front of us.

This soon became tedious, and when we glimpsed a little beach on the eastern bank we pulled in for breakfast. By the time we climbed back into the canoe, the curtains were lifting on an aggressively beautiful landscape. High, round mountains pushed upwards beside us. The morning sun periodically hid behind their peaks, while the river curled through a cliffed-gorge – carrying us with it.

Our only problem was the heat. The water around us glimmered in the sun, and the still-air of the gorge made it feel more like a vicious trap than a beautiful work of nature. Even the occasional gust of headwind was welcomed to cool us down. We drifted on, adamant that we were going to make the other side of the mountains by lunchtime. Eventually the river widened, the hills dropped out, and we turned around to see the mountains rising stoically behind us. We had made it – but we had to stop.

We found a suitable pontoon and as I jumped ashore my legs collapsed beneath me. I was exhausted. I lay, withering on the dock, as the sun beat down. So much for our long-term strategy.

Honestly, my memories of that day are little more than a hazy blur. I think that a combination of dehydration and exhaustion had scrambled the wires in my brain. Consequently, that evening, our progress was limited. The strain of the previous three days showed, and for the first time in the trip we bickered as we paddled. We pulled in at Shattemuc Yacht Club for the night and checked the map – 150 kilometres down, fifty to go. It could be done in one day, but it would be tough, and the conditions would have to be perfect. If the river was kind to us, we would be in New York by the following night. We went to bed excited, but uneasy.

oOo

Day Five

Our first glance at the river that morning left us speechless. A proper tailwind, at last. And we had a secret weapon. A sail, of sorts. It was a pretty rough piece of kit – a blue tarpaulin, a six-inch PVC pipe for a mast, and a wooden dowel rod for a boom – but we hoped it would provide us with a much-needed push downstream. At first though, we were disappointed by our progress. The wind was light, and paddling was difficult with the sail up. Any small wobble was magnified by the weight of the mast standing tall above us. Gradually though, the wind began to build, bit by bit, and our sail began to take shape. The river started chuckling cheerfully under the bows and soon we no longer needed to paddle, only steer occasionally when we were hit by an exceptional gust. The canoe sailed like a dream, accelerating beautifully and sliding smoothly down waves. So smooth, that not long after sailing under the Tappan-Zee Bridge, Rob fell fast asleep, leaving me all alone to guide us downstream, cruising through the miles.

The heat of the day began to build again, causing the horizon to blur and wobble in the haze, but through the mirage I began to make out a strange shape downstream, on the eastern bank. Unlike the rest of the horizon, this shape looked square and blocky, irregular and diffuse. When I realised what it was I was ecstatic.

'ROB! THE CITY!'

I woke Rob so rudely he nearly jumped out of the canoe with fright. But soon the pair of us were whooping with excitement. It was only a blur, but Manhattan seemed so tantalisingly close after such a long and gruelling journey.

Several hours later we sat on our haunches, staring at the skyline. The marina we had pulled into was on the New Jersey side of the river, giving a perfect view of our final destination. Between us and the finish lay just seven miles of water – a stone's throw compared to the journey that lay behind us. We would have made it if the wind had stuck around for another hour. But it had died, and with it our hopes of reaching New York that afternoon. Our paddling was no match for the incoming tide, and we could not go on. Below the dock, the water hosed past upstream, and we knew that any attempt to paddle against it would be futile. We would have to wait until five o'clock when the tide began to weaken, to make our final hellish push. A final push that would involve two hours of paddling through one of the busiest harbours in the world, at rush hour, with the sun racing us for the horizon.

We pushed off at five o'clock sharp, filled with excitement, quickly crossing to the

Manhattan side of the river. We tucked in as close to the bank as we dared, racing joggers along the towpath. To our left, the skyscrapers of the city. To our right, over the New Jersey side of the river, the sky reddened, its glimmer catching the sweat beginning to drip off our foreheads as we hunched over each stroke.

Soon we were hit with our first taste of the harbour – a high-speed ferry slicing clean across our path, and casting a huge wash over our bows. Suited commuters flashed past as we wobbled in their wakes. Soon we were surrounded by ferries, their wakes making the water wild and unpredictable. The canoe writhed beneath us as ferry horns blasted from all directions. They would charge past every thirty seconds, pausing at the bank to pick up commuters, before spinning around and heading back out into the river, a motorway of traffic that we would have to cross if we were to make our destination.

We powered on, our heads bent down like sprinters coming off starting blocks, every single exhausted sinew in my back tearing, ripping, to lay more weight on my paddle. We were giving it every last drop of energy left in our battered bodies. Ferries sped past, horns roaring as their high metal sides gleamed with the last rays of the blistering sun.

Our destination, *Pier 26*, came into sight in front of the World Trade Centre and we toiled towards it. That last stretch must have only taken about twenty minutes, but the pain made every second difficult. With every stroke we could see our final destination draw slowly closer. Eventually we reached it, paddling into the smooth water by the pier, and grabbing the side of the dock with our blister-covered hands. With one final effort we hauled the canoe out of the river, setting it gently onto the concrete dock.

New York stood there in all its glory. Office lights pricked brightly through the evening light that painted the skyscrapers dark-red. Rob and I didn't really have the energy to celebrate. We just turned and gave each other a sweaty bear-hug. And just for a second we must have made a pretty timeless image – two haggard Irish travellers, standing on the dock in New York, watching the Hudson flow by.

AVIVA DALE MARTIN

Aviva Dale Martin was born in Montreal and has lived most of her life in Vancouver, Canada. She studied Creative Writing, with Hugh MacLennan at McGill University, and later at the University of British Columbia. Aviva continued to write in a number of genres while engaged in a career in Early Childhood Education and Curriculum Design. She taught children's literature at Vancouver Community College, raised three children, and became a visual artist.

Now, in retirement from her profession, Aviva is enjoying the great pleasure of returning to extended and vigorous writing.

She has a particular interest in weaving character and description into interesting narratives. Her goal is to tell stories that are unique, provocative, and authentic, to explore the ways she can use language to further that objective, and to continue to experience the enjoyment she gets in her work.

COMMENDED
OUEN PRESS
SHORT STORY COMPETITION 2016

MANUELA
by Aviva Dale Martin

I.
Our landlady, Manuela, comes to collect the rent, receipt book in hand, and enters like a warrior. Her defences, fine-tuned to look like aggression, have been developed over many years of confrontation and haggling with ethnocentric tourists who think she should give them a better deal. For twenty-five dollars a day we get to hang out, cook, and sleep, but there are rules and there are limits. The outside rooftop, partially tiled and covered, which we want to consider our personal private space, can suddenly reconfigure as common property,

invaded by tenants from the suites below or by Manuela's daughters and their friends. Manuela has five daughters, a husband, a growing number of grandchildren, and a dog. Her dog, tied to the dusty jacaranda tree directly below our window, yelps into the night and I have to go downstairs and ask her, again, to move the bitch. There are sheets on lines that crisscross the yard and we may bring ours down once a week and exchange them for a clean set. Like her neighbours, Manuela burns leaves and branches and other debris when the clotheslines are empty. Sometimes the smoke is brown and enters my suite and I need to leave. In lieu of a housekeeping service there is a broom with mangled bristles and a metal dustpan whose bottom lip snarls and curls away from the floor when I try to feed it the dirt I have swept into piles.

'*Aviva, vengas, amiga,*' – 'come friend,' she calls to me from the yard three stories below where she and another lodger, Elizabeth, sit at her round rusted table.

I grab a cervesa and join them. I know the drill. Manuela has made something, this time ceviche. She wants to feed us and to hear how delicious it is. It is. The conversation is constant and vigorous. The topics are eclectic:

the local election, where to shop to get the freshest produce, our grandchildren. We talk about Gabriel, her husband, who is the principal of the local elementary school and who has come down with a mysterious affliction affecting the clarity of his speech and the stability of his muscles. On mornings when I see him leave for work, looking like he has emerged from a long night of drinking, I am surprised that he is still driving. I keep up with the mixture of Spanish and English until it exhausts me and I retreat upstairs, leaving Manuela and Elizabeth on their third beer.

At this time of day, the sun pinks my rooftop and pulls me into the sky, lifting me like the pelican that swooped over me while I swam earlier in the day. I am still in the glow of finding this place of warmth and ease. It is beyond anything we had seen or even hoped for in our search for accommodations on our arrival. We discovered it after we had traipsed the streets of the pueblo for three days looking for *'para rentar'* signs, climbing stone stairs to view dark or cramped or noisy rooms, thinking we might have to settle for something that was far from the beach or close to traffic. I stay outside until the red sun is gone and the clouds and my deck no longer reflect its light. Pacing the perimeter of the roof, which still gives off the day's heat and energy, I am marking my territory. The surrounding trees and hills fade into the night and into memories of trees and hills.

On this top floor of Manuela's enterprise there is only one suite and we are the only tenants. In the mid-90s, after the earthquake destroyed the local hotel, the residents of Melaque were given grants to build tourist accommodations on their properties. Manuela had a couple of suites constructed adjacent to her house, then five above, and finally, the year before we found it, our single, private penthouse. I call it a penthouse and I call it ours, both descriptors exaggerating the reality.

Melaque is a fishing town on Mexico's west coast between Puerto Vallarta and Manzanillo. It has been appropriated by tourists and expats from the US and especially Canada, to the mixed response of the local population. The tourist trade has brought in money, expansion, and civic improvements, advantageous to some but, as in all cases of foreign occupation, has altered the indigenous ambiance and lifestyle. It has exaggerated the economic gap. Manuela, and others who had property or commerce, have benefitted. But there are still peddlers working the beaches, families in shacks by the infested lagoon, beggars in the zocolo.

Inside our room, I start to cook our dinner. Bob has not returned from his swim. He'll be out of the water now. On the shore he will be watching the delicate reflecting harlequin fingers of the darkening ocean tide as it tries to reach the persistent soccer players, teams of families or of teenaged friends dancing along the edge of the sea and the edge of the day – agile figures silhouetted by the slight, remaining light. Sometimes the tide catches the ball and gives it back wet, sand-covered, but who cares. The fishers are pulling in their nets and the bathers, most from Guadalajara, who have been standing chest deep in the water for hours, extract themselves and their children and head for their food baskets and coolers on the shore.

o0o

II.

Two years later, February 2008, we return. Manuela smiles to see us again and greets us with hugs and news. Another grandchild, another daughter married. Gabriel has taken early retirement after a diagnosis of

Parkinson's. Long-time renters, Gus and Patricia, Spaniards who live in Ontario, are here again. Do we remember them? A Texan who was stalking Susana, one of her twin daughters, was extradited. After we take our bags upstairs we head for 'Hawaii' the largest grocery store in town, to stock up on essentials. It has more products than two years before and we can now buy peanut butter, sugar free juice, unflavoured yogurt, and granola.

We resume our gentle rhythmic Mexican pace – swimming everyday, Spanish lessons with Bonnie, Thursday market, early morning hikes in the surrounding hills before the sun sends us home or under beach umbrellas. Some days we sneak in a second swim at sunset or take our supper to the water to watch subtle changes in colour and mood as night replaces day. Some evenings we eat out at restaurants or taco stands with street seating, and move on to have ice-cream that exceeds any Italian gelato I've ever had.

When we cook at home we stick to simple vegetarian meals. Salads and bread, or stir-fry with pasta or rice. Everything is rinsed in our drinking water, poured from a multi-gallon tub wired into a contraption that dips till the water flows into glasses or jugs. I start the stove and add some of that drinking water to a pot for the pasta. I fill a plastic bowl with this water and dip each vegetable into it, then wipe the water off with paper towel, a laborious but necessary procedure to reduce the risk from tropical bacteria and parasites. At home, up north, I don't love to cook and I would find all the rinsing and wiping tedious and burdensome. I would have the radio noisy with talk or tunes. Distractions. But here, where the knives are blunt, the counters are too low, and the food needs to be carried over a kilometre from undersupplied grocery shops, I am content and the task becomes a meditation.

The tomatoes and cukes, onions and sweet peppers are a palette, large sweeps of colour to be sliced into other shapes or chopped small to create distinct staccato splashes in the glazed royal blue bowl. Often while I'm cooking I hear a neighbour, home from his day at sea, singing and cleaning fish – his family's daily catch. His clear tenor voice, sounding trained and classical and strong, sounding impossible, rises like a fountain from the desert that is his dusty bare impoverished landscape three stories below and enters my flat like wind.

We have been at Manuela's for three weeks

now. Things are not going well. I have had a cold for ten days, weak and sick, pulling myself around town or to the beach, unhappy. Bob spent last night on the bathroom floor, violently heaving, first the fish he had had for supper, then nothing, into the toilet at twenty-minute intervals. Manuela has entered our suite, begging us to move to one of the rooms below. We are packed and ready to leave tomorrow but she has miscalculated the dates and double booked the 'penthouse' this one night. Her new tenant paces the rooftop outside, raging. He enters and addresses us as though we are his collaborators. He doesn't blame us, he assures us, we are victims like he. He turns on Manuela; how can she run a business this way, he will find other lodging, he'll put the word out, her business will be ruined. He has invaded our space with his imperialism, his arrogance. He doesn't like the inconvenience of his situation so he has cracked his thin veneer of civility and become abusive. We lie on the bed, drained, impotent, watching this drama unfold on the stage of our living quarters. Manuela, getting nothing from our limp blank bodies, turns her pleading to him now, her voice rising to compete with his unceasing diatribe.

'*Por favor*, I have a bed for you, number five. Just one night. Tomorrow you move up here.'

We haven't the strength to participate, neither to tell him to get the hell out of our place nor to support Manuela nor to mediate nor to get the hell out ourselves. We only know we aren't going anywhere this night.

We had secured other lodging for the following week and we move there the next day. Unlike Manuela's on the outskirts, '*Vista Hermosa*' is in the middle of town and, although the hotel is large, about sixty units, our place is one of the only twelve suites away from traffic. We are fronting the ocean and looking over an expansive view from the palatial concrete balcony shared with the other third-floor occupants – 'snowbirds' – whose median age is about seventy. Here I can access what I need without exhausting my still sick self. The oceanscape and daily swims, at the beach at my door, revive me. Food is right across the street or down the block, tomales from the tomale-woman, salads at the American deli, bolillos, caso, vegetables from little grocery shops that line the main drag. A pared down, grateful, easy existence.

This dark lumbering hotel, three stories of stone and concrete, was built to accommodate

Mexican tourists from Mexico City and Guadalajara in the middle of the twentieth century when the town was a small fishing village just beginning to expand. It is across the street from the bus station and beside the town's bank. Our original plan was to go on a road trip after our three weeks with Manuela but I have no energy for that, so our discouraged little rental car waits for us, abandoned, on the street. Bob is also waiting. He calls this new place 'the old people's home' and detests it, even though, or perhaps because, he still is depleted after his night of purging. Travel for him has always been letting go of comforts and indulgences, changing perspective, discovering his strengths. In this hotel there is little opportunity for replacing convention, dropping contentment, examining assumptions. He feels like he has given up. And he has. He is done with this trip and his thoughts and spirit are already back home.

Bob's stomach is still protesting food so I go off by myself to find dinner, passing through the main floor of the hotel to get to the town centre. Unlike the suites that we and our compatriots occupy, most of the rentals comprise a couple of beds, a dresser, inside windows onto the courtyard and, usually turned on, a TV. These twelve dollars a night rooms surround a dark central rectangle containing a communal kitchen with a large gas stove, a fridge, a sink and plastic tables and chairs. When I return, I walk through the courtyard listening to a symphony of Spanish conversations, smell the tenants' food cooking on the shared stove, peek into the rooms through undraped glass where lodgers in undershirts or patterned dresses, on beds that blink and change colour in the aura of the omnipotent TVs, allow me to violate their privacy. I emerge on the other side of the tracks where the world opens up to the advantaged and I ascend the stairs. I cannot ignore the discrepancy. We are the privileged and I think this is part of why Bob dislikes this place so much. Vista Hermosa is named to describe the beautiful view that so few of us enjoy. There is so much disparity and our own complicity confronts us every day.

After two weeks we get into the car and set out shakily, driving north, a journey that is overdue and stale, and that unfolds and ends in discouragement and resignation. Only three days and a couple of hundred kilometres after we take to the road, we pay an exorbitant fee to change our flights and fly home, sixteen days early.

oOo

III.

I return to Melaque in January seven years later. After a few months of huddling and groping, months of myopic perceptions and slow weighty movements in the inert northern winter, I experience a dreamlike resurrection. The plane releases me and I shuffle in a long slow surreal line on the tarmac of the airport under an explosive sun. I drop my bags and search through them for shades and sunhat. I strip with urgency. My tender skin released from captive swaddling feels caressed, then sizzled.

Bob has stopped travelling, so now when I leave home I find other companions or I go alone. This time my youngest son, Noah, is with me for the first nine days. And when he leaves to resume his studies in England, my friend Rebecca and her partner Ivan will come.

We pass through immigration and the taxi takes us to Manuela as the day begins to disappear. The plan is to stash our suitcases and get to the beach for a swim before the sun sets. Noah lugs them up to our domain, sweating in this unaccustomed climate, while I say hello, hola, buenas tardes, and get the key. Manuela and I are both seven years older and I see in her, feel in her, when we hug, that something has slipped away. I sense it. Something of a diminishment, a thinning, not in a physical sense because she is larger, heavier. I think, this is not ageing alone that has happened.

Upstairs Noah puts the luggage on the beds and I walk across the room to pull back the curtains. I am stepping on dirt and on debris that has fallen from the palapa roof. There are tiny black ants, thousands of them, covering the counters, the table, and streaming up and down the walls. I look in the kitchen for a glass for some water but they are all covered in a layer of grease – and the shelves, pots, and implements are caked with grime. The beds at the end of the long room are ok with fresh linens and untainted blankets, so we can use those for the first night. But there is no clean area for unpacking. To free the beds for sleeping and to avoid contamination with the pervasive dirt, we move the still packed luggage out to the covered portion of the deck.

After a sunset swim, unshowered, we put

our wrinkled too-warm travel clothes over our salted bodies and walk into town for tacos. In the night my restless sleep is invaded by millions of dream-ants and nightmares of futile scrubbing.

When we return from breakfast in town we meet an Italian Canadian couple, Gus and Maria, the size and shape of two Volkswagen beetles, who are spending months in a suite below us. Like a weather report, they inform us of what we should expect from Manuela. She is 'lazy and truant'; there is her loud and persistent music, her lack of response to attend to repairs, her absenteeism. This last is not just an inconvenience to them but a moral judgment, embellished with stories of her early morning homecomings from all-night trysts while her 'poor sick' husband, Gabriel, languishes in a Parkinsonian hell. But she is my friend and I break away from the gossipers and continue upstairs to clean up the mess I have moved into. I wonder what they think they can expect for 250 pesos a day.

I look up the word for 'rag' in my Spanish dictionary – '*trapo*' – and spend the next few days cleaning my room. Manuela offers to do it but I decline. I only ask her to supply lots of rags, cleaners, ant poison, rubber gloves and a mask to provide an ineffectual barrier from the cleaning chemicals and the dirt. To do the work myself is an easy decision – in Manuela's latest incarnation she is incapable of delivering what I need and I can't move anything that I own into my room or use a dish or sit on a chair until I know that every crack and corner has been scrubbed and every ant exterminated. I start at the entrance and sanitise my way along.

With Noah's help it takes a couple of days, stopping for swims on the beach and meals in the pueblo, until at last the place is ours. We open the doors, safely walking in and out in bare feet. We bring in groceries and make our own breakfasts and lunches with shiny implements, eating off pristine plates. We wash the sea from our bodies in our disinfected shower, holding our breath for minutes to see if the hot will be delivered through the sluggish pipes. We gasp and scream out in jolting cold water if that hot, siphoned off by showers below, never arrives.

Noah and I fall into a parallel daily routine that feels like a dance as we pass each other in our activities and relate, from time to time, in a pas-de-deux. When I wake at around seven, Noah is usually already at the beach for an early swim. I begin to slowly enact a complex regimen, all my needs, all my indulgences, everything, detailed defined deliberate. It is unlike my morning routine back home where I am conscious of hurrying towards the day's appointments and endeavours, where I make phone calls and respond to emails while eating a quick unacknowledged breakfast. Here I unwrap the day without diversion, almost in slow motion, easily. It feels like turning the pages of a book, tearing them out, tossing them. I light a match for the gas stove to make my coffee measured into a funnel and poured in three stages. I toast bread in a frying pan, spread it with almond butter, jam, or honey and slice a fresh fruit on top. Before I take my breakfast outside, I wipe the counters thoroughly or there will be thirty ants at a banquet of honey and breadcrumbs, ants I will have to exterminate when I come back inside, and more victims on their way. I count out my day's supplements from hundreds of different capsules brought along to last my four weeks, a half suitcase full which empties over my stay to allow the transport home of a Mexican rug and silver jewellery.

Outside I pull a white plastic chair from under cover, where I had placed it last night to

shelter it from the dew. I set it at the edge of the roof with a pillow for my back, sit and put my feet up on the foot-high railing. My view is palm trees, bougainvillea, and coconut palms partly masking the neighbourhood of dusty roads, pink and yellow houses, and workers on rooftops. During my slow breakfast, the sun intensifies. I pause to put on my hat, peel off most of my clothing, and rub in sunscreen. After I have eaten and done a hand-wash with the pleasure of hanging it out in the bright sun and knowing that these water saturated things will be dry in a couple of hours, I change into my swimsuit and beach dress. In a large beach-bag I place items I will want for my time at the beach: book, glasses, sunglasses, money to buy water or a coconut, possibly guacamole or fries, sunblock fifteen, sunblock thirty, sunhat, three towels, snacks, pen and paper.
Meanwhile Noah has returned, prepares and eats his breakfast and sets up outside to begin his work. His doctoral thesis is due in June so he works five or six hours every day. In contrast to ageing obsessive me, with my ridiculously bulky bag, Noah comes and goes unencumbered, wearing his bathing suit and carrying only a small towel, swimming goggles, and a water bottle.

At the beach I deposit my stuff at one of the umbrella'd tables, say '*Hola*' to Miguel who will bring me a fresh coconut to drink after I have done my first swim, and I head for the sea. The tourists I sometimes chat with are distressed when I leave my bag unattended on the beach.

Between swims I watch the fishers mending nets, casting lines, swimming out to their boats, returning with their catch. At home at sea. Amphibian. They are old men with leathery skin and lifetimes of repetition; their lives an encyclopaedia of tides and weather and fish runs. And young men, shirtless, muscular, loquacious or unspeaking, determined to carry on their legacy, attached to the rhythms of their ancestors. They push out to sea and disappear behind the sun, silhouettes, intense in their labours, beautiful on the water – gliding over, glimmering, gone. Later, their boys and grandsons, home from school and right into the boats to study this trade of dwindling returns.

This year there is an odd appearance in the water. Most days, after a few minutes of swimming, a small fish bumps my leg, then two, three, five minnow-sized fish are bumping into me, and within a few seconds there are scores. This phenomenon is, and will remain, a mystery. I try to make sense of it, ask questions of other swimmers, and ask Miguel and other waiters – what are the fish doing? Nibbling dead skin, sustenance, from our bodies? Bumping lice off themselves? What kind of fish are they? Nobody has information. I look for a pattern. Are there more when the water is cooler, at different times of the day, closer to shore or farther out? I find no consistency, only that they are always in groups, swarms, that they bombard the legs, rarely the arms or above the waist. And when they follow me into shore and I have attained shallow enough water, they turn around and leave as one. Noah gets used to the fish, even misses them when occasionally they don't show up. But I never do. They disturb me and I lose the ease and distraction of swimming. When they are not there, I am waiting for them. When they show up, I race into shore to get rid of them. This year there are far fewer pelicans diving for fish in these waters and that may be a clue to this uncanny blight.

After Noah has done four or five hours of work on his thesis and I have sat under a beach umbrella, been in and out of the water, passed the time drinking from a coconut, eating peanuts or guacamole, reading, reviewing my Spanish, maybe drawing or writing, we reunite in the late afternoon. We spend the rest of the day together, sometimes for another swim, sometimes just to let the sun set, usually to walk into town for dinner. We may go back to the taco stand where Noah is adventurous and often chooses tongue – *'lingua'*, liver – *'higado'*, or other organ meats, and I feel a silly pride in him and his adventurous tastes. We may walk around the zocolo for a while, like half the townsfolk, minding everybody's business and eating flan or other pastries that are baked at home by villagers and brought to the centre to sell.

We watch the milling, the families whose children dressed in pink organdy or gabardine, barely able to toddle, make their way around the square, arms outstretched for balance or raised straight up to clutch a finger of a teenage brother or a grandmother. We watch a young father engage with his baby while the mother chats with her friends beside them. The four adolescent boys perched on the back of a single bench, relaxed and confident in each other's company, exude their virgin sexual energy in this square which has been their rock and their world since they were the toddlers not very long ago. We may pick up some bread or fruit at Hawaii, may fill three or four bags, because Noah is strong and game to carry all of them the kilometre home. Once, when we were in Italy, I remarked on how well we travelled together.

'Yup, my muscle and your money,' was his quick response.

At home, almost every night, there is the incongruence of a downloaded episode of Seinfeld out under the stars.

Gus and Maria have friends over most evenings after she has spent full days in the kitchen making pizza and pasta from scratch while he tends Manuela's garden, stopping me to complain about her 'sloth' and the rent when I walk by. The other rooms fill and empty, and Gus and Maria complain about the noise and the excessive numbers of people occupying the small rooms – weekend families from inland Mexico.

A couple of times Maria invites Noah and me to a lunch of pizza and grilled vegetables and tells me where and when to buy the best fish. Italy in Mexico, the best of all possible worlds. Sometimes I see her in the zocolo at night, sitting on a bench with three other women in deep musical incessant Italian discourse. I yearn a little for that familiar female group friendship that I have back home, and had here in the past when Manuela was accessible and chatted with her women friends and her tenants.

But now Manuela is in and out, living a different kind of life from the one I observed years before when the scene had been teeming with the comings and goings of neighbours, of friends, of her daughters and their children. Now they are absent and I do not ask, sensing that Manuela does not want to explain, sensing that there have been quarrels, maybe estrangements. She easily tells me that her husband, sick and dependent, is now living with his sister in the colonial city of Colima, several hours drive from Melaque, to be close to the hospital there. But she is silent about her night-time activities, and I don't get to tell her that I am happy that events and the judgments of others have not defeated her; that she retains the spirit to allow new things in her life.

Rebecca and Ivan arrive one day and Noah leaves the next. I am excited to introduce them to Mexico, especially to Melaque and all I have discovered here. They are renting a room below me on the second floor, and will share the kitchen and terraza at my place. I inspect their room carefully before they arrive – the shower works, the windows open. I get Manuela to replace the torn curtains. Everything is clean. But from the start there are problems – the toilet is blocked. This is their first trip to Mexico and their expectations are based on brochures and promos of timeshares and resorts. They find it impossible to communicate with Manuela. I know she can speak and understand enough English, but her moods fluctuate and she is not in a compliant disposition when they arrive.

'*Si*, I have call the plumber. He will come soon.'

She gives them the key to an empty room at the far end of the floor so they can use its toilet. She knows how to be just accommodating enough so that her tenants won't leave and, on her good days, she can be amenable. But, until I intervene she is at the low end of the scale with these new arrivals. 'Soon', I know, can mean some time in the next week and that once she has given them the other room key she feels she has solved the problem. I insist she call the plumber again to give us an exact time and I follow her to listen while she does this, relieved to hear the word *'emergencia'* included in her negotiation to get him to come sooner. Eventually my friends are comfortable and enjoying their holiday, the beach, the restaurants, the day trips. But they are never enamoured with my lovely Melaque, and continue to wonder at my appreciation of Manuela.

When they leave I think I will be happy to be alone for the last five days of my trip, a short period of relative solitude. But I find that living with myself is cheerless and fraught. The days are long. I am lonely and uncertain, especially when I come home from the beach in the late afternoon and am faced with heading out for supper alone. Some evenings I stay home with the simplest of meals – nuts and tomatoes, or cucumbers and cheese, choosing to eat minimally, inadequately, rather than to face my anxiety about making the trek into town to find a restaurant on my own. On those nights I can't even find the enthusiasm to carry my food to the beach to watch the sun go down while I eat. Even though she knows I am alone, Manuela does not seek me out nor make herself available. I miss her. I miss everyone. I wonder if I had offended her in some way or if I am just another well-off tourist from a more advantaged world, from a luckier life. Am I, also, just an economic necessity?

But when I leave she is there to send me on my way. Our eyes connect and her smile is genuine.

'You come back next year?'

And I wonder if there are other places along the west coast that I might want to try. Or maybe the Yucatan. Someone was saying that West Jet has a direct flight from Vancouver to Cancun during the winter months. I tell her I will let her know.

PREVIEW

We are delighted to be able to preview a short travel story by Michael Connor whose collection of travel pieces is scheduled to be published by Ouen Press in 2018.

MICHAEL CONNOR

Michael Connor has been a freelance writer for a number of years, specialising in food, travel and crime. He is hotel-school trained and has spent lengthy periods in Africa (including Zimbabwe and Sierra Leone), China, Greece, the former Republic of Yugoslavia, the Caribbean and the UK.

Michael enjoys a broad range of music, an endless selection of movies, off-the-main-routes travel and has a particular affinity with Africa. He reads a great deal, mainly contemporary literature, and finds 'street-food' and ethnic dishes more appealing than formal dining – carnivals more entertaining than the summer ball.

Currently he is editing a travel memoir from his time spent working in the hospitality industry around the world. Along with writing a novella set in a fine-dining restaurant.

Michael is a member of English PEN which promotes free speech, human rights and a greater understanding through literature

FLIGHTS OF FANCY
by Michael Connor

It must have been at the end of the 1970's – I was a partner in an offshore company running small-scale casino operations. Highly successful, but a year or two in and it was all becoming a bit mundane. I wanted more fun, broader horizons. So, on a quiet, rainy afternoon I dictated a sales letter and, with a secretary, began faxing it to random opportunities around the globe. The scatter-gun sales approach. Expressions of interest came back, with firm invitations from a company in Canada and another in India – not bad!

The winter had turned cold and the thought of some Indian sun was all it took to persuade my fellow director, Rob, to book the flights. My first trip to India, Bombay – as the city was then known, and I am told this is still the case with many of the locals rejecting the name, Mumbai.

Snow banked white on each side of the motorway approaching Heathrow. The first fall of winter – heavy, deep and yet to be dirtied by flying slush. Crowds of ticket-holders, intent on leaving, churned around the departure area, stopping abruptly every time the flight information board clicked-clacked over to reveal more news to prolong the stranded, in which Rob and I were becoming unwilling participants.

The board-strip stated it, the girl behind the desk said it, and a jumbo-jet number of rejected passengers confirmed it. The British Airways flight to Bombay – our flight – was clearly cancelled. At times like these it is no good flocking with the rest of the sheep. And being a shepherd is also of little benefit. No. Take on the role of the dog and sniff out an advantage. Analysing the situation, not focusing simply on one's own predicament, it became immediately apparent that departures were being announced and the roar of jet engines could clearly be heard. So what was our problem? Why weren't we flying?

Airline personnel were in hiding, not venturing out for fear of being devoured by the demanding hoards. But patience and agility finally paid dividends. Cap removed, head down, no eye contact, a young member of the airport staff was skirting around the far wall, having entered from one door and heading by an indirect route to disappear via another. The youngest had been picked for the job nobody else wanted – whatever that was. A moment before he disappeared, thinking he had made a clear run, we blocked his way.

Well it transpired that planes could take off but not land, and that British Airways had nothing left on the ground. Our flight would have been arriving from somewhere else, but couldn't. Our best bet was to locate another Bombay flight with a carrier who had a plane sitting on the tarmac, and get our tickets changed. Not bad, no twisting of arms necessary. Information provided at speed, before he could be identified and corralled by the masses.

The weather was not going to improve, so Iraqi Airways departing in six hours – the only option – got our attention, and was pleased to assign us their last two seats. Not a direct flight, but only a short stop-over in Baghdad. We had planned to arrive a day early to compensate for jet-lag, so our meeting arranged for commencement of business Monday morning would not be at risk.

How we came to get the two seats by the emergency exit with a clear expanse of leg room I didn't know, but it was not time to look a gift horse etc. In fact the space, if measured, was sufficient I'm convinced to park a large Shire. Both Rob and I carried far from slim-line briefcases, having taken some care not overload our suitcases. Pre-laptop and Power Point, a complete set of our operating layouts had been crammed in, everything heavy had been packed in our carry-on bags. The extra space was again lucky, as the overhead lockers were already stuffed full with hand luggage from three rows back. A good fifty per cent of the passengers were dressed in Arab garb and their sheer volume of packages, bundles and other paraphernalia made our excess appear trivial and would have made many a souk-trader envious.

Rob had fought his way through the feeding frenzy of roaming fast-food fans during our prolonged Heathrow experience, twice, to ensure that he would not be starved into eating the in-flight fare. And had secreted away a flask-bottle of single malt, in case the religious laws prevented the service of alcohol, a packet of crisps and a pre-packed sandwich of pap bread and questionable content. Rob knew what he liked – his local football team (which in recent times has gained fame for sliding into receivership) and a plate of egg and chips. Me, on the other hand, always eager to experience everything on offer.

The take-off was smooth; the cabin crew were female and appeared to think the chat-up lines from Rob were amusing. We left on time and the London lights sparkled in the dark like fallen stars. It was not long before the smell of meths and a waft of pungent cooking spice alerted my nostrils to the imminent arrival of dinner. Time passed and no food trolley seemed to be heading in our direction despite the atmosphere filling with middle-eastern promise. So before the loos became in demand, as is always the case once the food carts have been packed away, I decided to pee and reconnoitre the activity en route. The extinguished seat-belt sign seemed to have signalled to everyone on board, the absolute requirement to mingle and rearrange one's life, rather than giving permission if essential. Then I saw it. It was a first and something, despite the hundreds of thousands of miles I have flown since, I have never witnessed again. Half-way along the aisle behind us, a family was hard at work preparing dinner. Maybe they knew something that Rob had only suspected.

The father, squatting in his robes, was vigorously pumping a hissing primus stove, typically used for preparing coffee, whilst his wife, with the artistry of an experienced blender, added ingredients to the hot pan. Further on, others followed the same pursuits – it was rapidly taking on the look of a Scout jamboree cook-out but with recipes, meticulously created, that would not be alien in the early rounds of *Masterchef*. As I retraced my steps along the aisle, drowsy children and over-excited teenagers were being fed steaming morsels wrapped in flatbread.

Back at my seat I was confronted by the back of Rob's head, as he stared down at the area of floor in front of our seats that had been empty a few minutes earlier when I set off on my short expedition. A passenger wearing a *galabiyya* was, with clear irritation, pushing our bags aside to make space as he unrolled a prayer mat. Then, to Rob's amazement the man knelt and began praying at Rob's feet. Hands raised, eyes staring directly into Rob's face on each upward motion. In procession, much to Rob's on-going embarrassment, the ritual appeared continuous from then on, only the identity of the devout believer changing.

The flight, as far the cabin crew was concerned, did not seem anything out of the ordinary. Food was served. I have to admit however, what the small selection of dishes held I can't honestly recall. But I am sure I ate it, as I am equally sure Rob did not.

Our first landing was no more than fifteen or so minutes late, which was encouraging. However, as the wheels came to a standstill the pilot was apologetic over the intercom informing us that, due to fog in Baghdad, we had been diverted and had now touched down in Damascus. The wait was endless, punctuated only by prayer. Food, drinks and the circulation of air were all in short supply and the heat was compounded by the reappearance of the primus stoves. Eventually, even the Arab contingent on board, who seemed to have taken everything very much as a matter of the 'only to be expected', began to show their displeasure as the first hour became the second. Our thirst was quenched a further hour into the wait when the cabin crew distributed water and the assurance that the flight would be commencing very shortly, and that we had been redirected to Amman before flying directly to Bombay – as Baghdad was still cloaked in fog.

We may not have been at the Jordanian capital's main airport, but it would be a generous comment to say it was somewhat sparse, with facilities that were approaching airstrip in sophistication. Stepping down onto the runway, it was then only a short walk across the tarmac to a low level building that contained what could have been a transit lounge or an area that serviced all passengers regardless. But to say it was designed by someone who had previously specialised in English church-halls would convey an appropriate appearance.

The two staff on duty, and there were only two, smiled and were keen in their *gahwaji* role, to offer the tiny shwarma-style savories or very sweet peanut sticks, small handless cups of Arabic coffee, flavoured with cardamom, and larger glasses of water as is the custom. As soon as one traditional three-stringed tray was empty it was immediately replenished. Rob partook of nothing, placing himself strategically under the ceiling fan and feeling he had been cast back to a scene only available in the director's cut of *Casablanca*. I think long-before 'passengers flying to Bombay, India should re-board their plane,' was announced, which referred to everyone in the lounge, Rob had long since dived below his threshold of acceptable pain. Had there been an aircraft on the ground with any type of English wording on the fuselage he would have paid every penny he had, and hocked his watch, to have obtained a seat.

'Keep smiling,' I told him, 'you could be back in the UK in three foot of snow.'

As sweat poured down his face, the salt turning his eyes into bloodshot holes, and his shirt clung to his torso, he seemed unable to raise the smile I considered a joke of this calibre clearly warranted.

The bag strap was cutting into my shoulder and my resistance had all but ebbed away, when the porter, smiling, offered to place my heavy bag in the hold, as I walked across to rejoin the plane. I insisted it was not possible as all my luggage had already been checked.

'You give it to me, I put it in the hold. No problem. Much easier,' he assured me.

Complying defied logic. But it was unbearably heavy, truly I did not want to carry it. If a fuss was caused, it might be that it would not be permitted back on board at all and I would be made to leave it behind. It was ridiculously heavy, but the original intention had been to place it on the plane and not to move it again until arrival at our destination. I conceded and watched the porter take it to the open undercarriage. As good as his word he appeared to place it inside. I continued to monitor the comings and goings until the hold doors were finally closed, at which point I was made to hurry. Apparently, it was now urgent that the plane took off without delay.

Enquiries into our ETA were not very forthcoming. The best we could achieve was 'We are expected to be on time, Sir.' So we settled in for the long haul across the Indian Ocean, Rob feeling much more relaxed with the reduced bouts of worship. The passenger numbers had thinned as some had made their onward connections from each of our impromptu ports of call.

My shallow sleep was ended by a change in the engine tone and some serious noise from the undercarriage. Not the sort of sounds I had come to expect a short time into a flight that was expected to last for a number of hours. I had dozed, certainly, but had not drifted into a near comatose state long enough for us now to be descending into a landing pattern over Bombay.

'Will all passengers please return to their seats and fasten your seat belts,' an authoritative voice on the intercom instructed.

'What's happening?' I asked, grabbing the arm of a passing stewardess.

'We are landing,' she replied in a voice that seemed equally confused and rushed to move on to clear away and secure.

'I thought we were going straight to Bombay?'

'So did I. But it seems the fog has lifted and were are going back to pick up the passengers who were due to join us in Baghdad,' she said before disappearing behind a curtain.

The touch down and turn around that we were promised, compared to the previous excursion to earth, was in a relative sense accurate – only a few minutes short of six hours.

'We will not be disembarking at this time, as we expect to be given a slot to leave shortly,' was the message repeated on the hour, every hour.

Had we not spent six hours in Baghdad we would not have spent, on arrival in Bombay, the next six hours sitting once more in our seats without refreshment or any cooling system other than the open doors. At six a.m., minutes before the Iraqi Airways flight from London to Bombay landed at its final destination, the porters at Bombay airport staged a strike. No baggage could be unloaded and no steps would be wheeled up to the aircraft to permit passengers to transfer to the airport building. It took until lunch-time for the airline, the airport authority and the porters to negotiate pushing the tubular steel steps the twenty-five yards from where they had been abandoned up to the open door of the plane. Hostesses with hard to achieve smiles thanked everyone, as they stumbled forward to the exit, for flying with Iraqi Airways.

The queue, which Rob and I were pleased to be near the front of, moved quickly, as European passport holders presented their documentation, and only slightly slower for Indian nationals. I had begun to sweat. Rob, passport in hand and an eye on a stand offering cold drinks a short distance away in the arrivals lounge, was throwing everything he had left into achieving that goal. I was searching my pockets again, and then for a third time with absolutely no success.

By the time I was confronted with the smiling face at the desk, it had dawned on me. I smiled back.

'Passport,' spoken in English with a local lilt.

I had nothing to place in the extended hand.

'It is in my bag,' I explained.

'Well can I have it please. Your passport must be stamped on entry,' he laboured patiently, not understanding why I was not understanding.

'My bag is in the hold.'

He looked at me now as if I were a stowaway or a member of the Red Brigade.

'That is not possible. Stand over there,' he pointed to an area outside a small office and at the same time nodded to one of the guards who were casually hanging around. They were armed and I complied, knowing I would be able to sort the predicament very quickly once the remainder of the arrivals had passed on their way. It took an hour before I again became the focus of attention.

It was difficult to argue the logic of my lack of passport.

'It is not possible for your passport to be in your luggage. Luggage is checked in before you go through passport control and your passport is checked again as you show your boarding pass.'

'True. But my hand-luggage, which contained my passport, was placed in the hold by a porter when we were on the ground in Damascus. No Amman. Yes, when we landed in Amman.'

I could see this explanation was not moving my position forward.

Finally, after numerous attempts to persuade the group of officers who had formed around me, now with little else left to do, of the true status of my passport, I came up with the answer.

'I will go through to the arrivals lounge, get my bag, come back here and you can then stamp my passport, inspect my visa, and everyone is happy,' I ventured.

'No.'

I did not bother to question the reply.

'OK. I will go through and get my bag. You send one of the armed officers with me and if I try to run off he can shoot me,' I offered.

'No'

The possibility of my remaining on the tarmac for the rest of my life now seemed to be looming.

'My colleague is in the arrival lounge, he can get my bag and he has a passport, so no problem.'

'This is not possible.'

'Why is this not possible?' I asked peeping between the green-clad men surrounding me, for a seat where I could sit and grow old.

'The porters have refused to unload the luggage. Your friend will go to his hotel and when the luggage has been unloaded, it will be sent there," one of the more forthcoming officers informed me.

The actuality of the situation then began to seep through. If my hand-luggage happened to be linked to my checked baggage it would be sent to the hotel. Rob would then need to bring it back from the hotel for me to be able to be permitted entry. Worse, it is left unidentified, finds its way back to the UK or is lost forever.

'Will they be unloading soon?'

'This shift is on strike and they have left. The new shift is not due to start until 6 p.m.'

'So I have to wait here until 6 p.m. before we can even start to sort this out?' I asked.

'That will happen if the new shift does not go on strike when they arrive,' he shrugged.

The new shift did unload the luggage and without any fuss one of the guards wandered over to the plane and collected it, before indifferently sending me on my way in a death defying taxi ride to Juhu Beach and the hotel.

We did not get a contract, but everyone we met was nice and treated us well, and I had made my first journey to a country I now love. British Airways reinstated our tickets for the homeward flight, allowing Rob a sigh of relief.

I did very well playing *teen pathi*, a local card game similar to three-card brag, each evening after dinner, having spent seven hours perfecting the game, and losing two cartons of duty-free cigarettes, sitting on the steps of passport control with the guards while waiting for the plane to be unloaded.

Rob (not his real name by the way) did not lose too much weight as the hotel served dishes in their restaurant that vaguely resembled something he might have eaten in the UK if nothing else was on offer. Although, much to everyone's amazement, he was persuaded to eat a plate of curry on the last day – but that is another chapter.

OTHER PUBLICATIONS
FROM OUEN PRESS

CODY, THE MEDICINE MAN AND ME
by Alan Wilkinson — a rites of passage story about a middle-aged man who takes a trip across the USA that transforms into the ultimate voyage of personal discovery. Attempting to establish the truth of his baffling ancestry, and struggling to prepare himself for a reunion with his estranged twin brother - old rivalries quickly resurface. **A showdown brews – but ultimately only one of the brothers can ride off into the sunset.**

MAY ALL YOUR NAMES BE FORGOTTEN
by Michael Connor — a fast moving crime thriller set in south London, containing as many pointers for budding telesales-staff, prepared to break the rules, as it does for the ordinary citizen seeking to avoid being hustled.

LAST CALL & OTHER SHORT STORIES
including Ouen Press Short Story Competition Winners 2015 – take the reader on countless memorable journeys that reflect that vast, often unfathomable melting-pot of human emotions and intention.

Made in the USA
San Bernardino, CA
12 May 2017